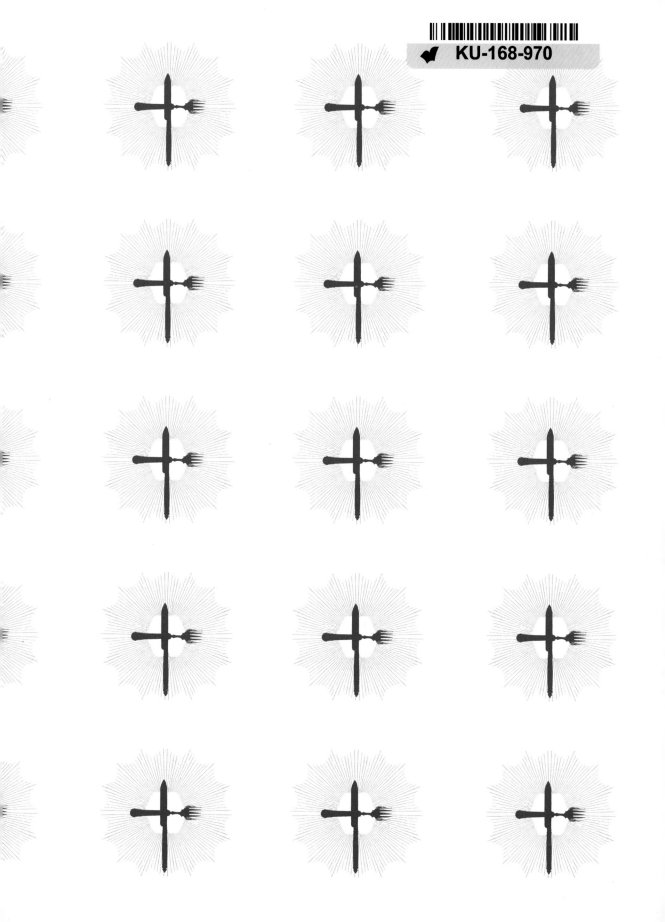

LET THERE BE
MEAT

LET THERE BE
MEAT

120 GLORIOUS RECIPES
celebrating the joy of
TRUE
BARBECUE

THE HOLY COW

AMEN

OUR HEAVEN SENT
COLLECTION OF
TEARS OF JOY
AND WHEN THEY REALISED THEY
WERE AVAILABLE BY THE BOTTLE THEIR
SOULS SHONE BRIGHT

CONTENTS

SCOTT JAMES

IN THE BEGINNING...

Like lightning from heaven itself, Red was struck. The people of Britain knew nothing of *True Barbecue*. Of prime cuts, smoked low and slow, infused with flavour and worthy of worship. These poor souls were ignorant of glazes and rubs so glorious that angels wept tears of joy. They had been cursed to endure a plague of sad sausages and bog-standard burgers.

SOMETHING MUST BE DONE
The people must be saved

But even the almighty couldn't act alone, so Red recruited disciples Scott Munro and James Douglas. In these two he saw passion and determination of biblical proportions.

Scott had spent his childhood in South Africa, where 'braai' was an integral part of his culture. His love of barbecue was honed further by frequent trips across the southern United States, where he tackled the behemoth beef ribs and brisket of Texas, the baby backs of Memphis, and the pulled pork of the Carolinas. James was a dedicated foodie and meat lover, too. His own exploits would lead to the development of Red's own sweet and smoky Kansas City BBQ sauce which graces the tables of all of Red's restaurants.

Together they saw a truly exciting opportunity: to bring their own take on cross-regional authentic smokehouse barbecue to the UK, converting the masses into True Believers.

The first Red's opened its doors in September 2012 in Leeds, welcoming an eager congregation and immediately operating at capacity. The pit was headed up by Scott's childhood friend Clinton Britz, whose experience as a classically trained chef helped in the development of 'The Good Book', Red's menu.

The gospel of True Barbecue spread quickly and within 18 months a second beacon of hope greeted the masses of Manchester. Soon outposts began popping up across the country and the flock swelled. Before long, believers from Scotland to London began to turn to Red's for salvation and plead for their own place of worship.

The sheer joy that is found in the preparation, cooking and devouring of the glorious food within these pages means that you can share a little True Barbecue heaven at home. We hope you enjoy every minute and mouthful. Amen.

#LetThereBeMeat

THE RISE, FALL AND RISE AGAIN OF TRUE BARBECUE

Paul Sturtevant, Believer, US citizen and Professor of Medieval Studies

Barbecue to most Brits means cremating sausages and burgers directly over hot coals, usually under an umbrella.

To an American, particularly one from the southern United States, 'barbecue' is a very specific word. It does not mean simply the act of cooking al fresco, but refers to a specific set of dishes, cooked in a very particular way and traditionally served at informal, social gatherings. It is a style of food that has inspired passion, and even obsession, among its devotees. And though it is a food that has been served by presidents at formal state dinners, it retains its rural, working-class roots and a sense of being old-fashioned, unpretentious, fun-loving and honest.

True barbecue - that is food cooked low and slow over smoke - was born at the intersection of Native American, African and European cultures, and, like America itself, it is shot through with the histories of co-operation, conflict and oppression.

While many 'cue aficionados in different states may lay claim to being the first to create barbecue, the true birthplace lies just outside the barbecue belt - Virginia. Virginia society barbecues were raucous, all-day affairs that usually culminated in copious drinking and dancing. Soon, pig mixed with politics. It was in the Virginia colony that the first barbecues as political rallies were held, during which candidates would 'treat' their constituents and supporters with liquor and food.

Barbecue spread south from Virginia into the Carolinas as frontier families began to move along the eastern edge of the Appalachian Mountains, seeking new lands to farm. These first backcountry barbecues were crude attempts to reconstruct Virginia society, but despite humble beginnings, barbecuing culture had begun to take hold, and from there it spread across the South.

Around this time, thanks to the African population in America, barbecue took on many of its particular characteristics from African cooking techniques and flavours, including sour-spicy sauces made from hot peppers and citrus juice.

Following the Civil War and emancipation, barbecue culture became the standard mode of community building and collective celebration across a wide swathe of the US - school celebrations, building of the railroads, town-boosting land sales, social club gatherings, church get-togethers; you name it. Whole animals would be slaughtered and cooked over an open pit for all to enjoy.

And then something happened at the turn of the 20th century, which fast-tracked the distinct regional characteristics of barbecue and took it from field to fork. Changes in the production and packing of meat, a demographic shift of people moving from the countryside into the cities, and increasing ease of travel made barbecue a commercially viable enterprise, and so the very first barbecue restaurants were born.

Pitmasters could now choose what animals they wanted to cook, or even what specific cuts of the animal to use. Typically they chose what was plentiful (and therefore cheap) in their region. In Texas, they went from barbecuing whole cows, to only the forequarters, to finally only the brisket or ribs. In the Carolinas, some pitmasters opted to use only the shoulders of the pig, while in the Midwest, they went for the ribs. Eastern North Carolina is the only significant holdout: to this day they still barbecue their hogs whole.

'Cue joints sprang up across the country wherever there were hungry people to feed. These restaurants and their pitmasters became local institutions, and in their experimentation and competition with one another for the tastes and dollars of their customers, they invented the traditional regional distinctions that divide the South to this day.

In 1940, two brothers built a pit and served barbecue to hungry travellers. Their story is not remarkable - roadside barbecue stands had been opening across the country as America's first national fast food - but the names of these brothers were Richard and Maurice McDonald, and their restaurant was McDonalds Bar-B-Q.

The duo quickly realised that the majority of their profits came from selling hamburgers and so re-tooled themselves into the assembly-line industrial-food restaurants that blanket the world today. Prior to the rise of the burger joint, barbecue was the national fast food. The legions of new burger chains out-competed and displaced most roadside barbecue joints to the backyard.

In the years immediately following World War II, there was a massive movement of people into the American suburbs. The American middle-class fantasy was born and, for many, your own barbecue in the backyard. These mid-century barbecues were not the steel-and-propane behemoths of today's suburban barbecue, but permanent structures of brick and mortar. Enthusiastic home cooks used them to prepare hamburgers, hot dogs (which became popular during wartime rationing), chicken, steaks, corn or anything else they could get their hands on. Due to their similarity to barbecue pits, it was generally accepted that what they were doing was, in fact, 'barbecuing', and the social events they held in their back yards were 'barbecues'.

And then, the final blow.

Companies began bottling sugary, tomato-based sauces infused with smoke flavouring. These were labelled 'barbecue sauce' and sold in grocery stores. Suddenly, the home cook no longer needed a pitmaster to achieve a vague facsimile of barbecue flavour, and 'barbecue' became redefined as any food flavoured with that sauce. No pitmaster, no special equipment, no expertise necessary - just meat in a sauce.

But all was not lost. Barbecue retrenched to its original purpose - bringing people together. Over the course of the 1980s the first of the great barbecuing competitions were founded. And their popularity exploded, creating a regional and national circuit that attracted pitmasters from hundreds of miles away to do battle.

The same regional peculiarities and artisanal nature of barbecue that caused it to fail in the face of mass-industrial fast food made it a perfect competition cuisine - part sport, part religion. Today there are over 500 barbecue cook-offs in the United States and the largest and most prestigious of these is the Memphis in May festival, held on the banks of the Mississippi each year. It hosts 250 barbecuing teams - gathered by invitation only - who compete in a strictly pork-only competition and watched by over 90,000 visitors.

And so we return to where we started - American barbecue has now taken off in Britain. But unlike a number of other recent food-fads, American barbecue brings with it a cultural tradition with deep roots. And far from being accidental, there are a number of cultural reasons why barbecue is popular now, both in terms of what it is, but also in what it symbolises as a counter-cultural icon.

Over the past 15 years Britain has gone through a culinary renaissance. There's a newfound love for rural life, a break from modernity and escape from the grind of city living and the virtual, manufactured world. We've rekindled a desire for hand-crafted and artisanal foods, we have a punkish rejection of calorie counting and a nerdy, obsessive devotion to appreciating food. Barbecue exemplifies this fantasy and more. *Being a British foodie is no longer an exercise in disappointment, nor is it rare.* Amen.

CELEBRATING REGIONAL DIFFERENCES

The regional differences are unique characteristics of American barbecue and for us it's what makes it the most interesting food style in the world. Nowhere else do you get such passion and belief. There's no wonder that there's an oft-repeated saying in the South: there are three subjects that must be either avoided in casual conversation or defended to the death: religion, politics and barbecue.

THE REGIONAL BATTLE LINES
have been drawn.

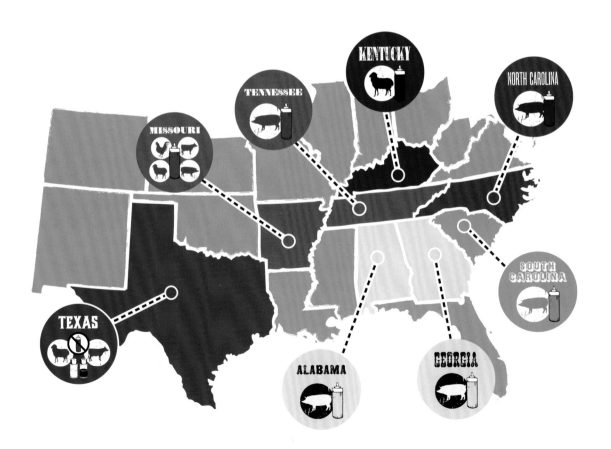

EAST NORTH CAROLINA

Meat/cut of choice: the whole hog, finely chopped

Sauce or rub: sour/spicy vinegar-pepper sauce without sugar and tomato

WEST NORTH CAROLINA

Meat/cut of choice: pork shoulder, finely chopped

Sauce or rub: similar to East but with the addition of tomato in the sauce

SOUTH CAROLINA

Meat/cut of choice: pork shoulder, pulled

Sauce or rub: mustard-based sauce

GEORGIA AND ALABAMA

Meat/cut of choice: pork

Sauce or rub: Georgia - ketchup and molasses-based sauce; Alabama - white barbecue sauce of mayonnaise and vinegar

KENTUCKY

Meat/cut of choice: mutton

Sauce or rub: Worcestershire-based black sauce

TENNESSEE

Meat/cut of choice: pork ribs

Sauce or rub: dry rub, often consisting of dark brown sugar, coriander, mustard powder, paprika and cayenne. The sauce is sweet, mixing tomato and molasses

MISSOURI - KANSAS CITY

Meat/cut of choice: pork and beef ribs, brisket, pork shoulder, chicken, ham, turkey

Sauce or rub: thick, sweet tomato and molasses-based sauce

MISSOURI - ST. LOUIS

Meat/cut of choice: St. Louis cut pork rib and pork steak

Sauce or rub: thick, sweet tomato and molasses-based sauce

EAST TEXAS

Meat/cut of choice: beef ribs, pork shoulder and pork ribs

Sauce or rub: sweet tomato and molasses-based sauce

CENTRAL TEXAS

Meat/cut of choice: beef brisket and hot links/hot guts (sausages)

Sauce or rub: salt and pepper rub, typically with no sauce or only a thin tomato-vinegar sauce

WEST TEXAS

Meat/cut of choice: beef, cooked quickly over open mesquite fires

Sauce or rub: none

SOUTH TEXAS

Meat/cut of choice: lamb, goat and cow's head, cooked barbacoa-style

Sauce or rub: none

NOW LET'S GET DOWN

WHAT EXACTLY IS GRILLING?

This is the most direct and straightforward of all cooking methods. It uses a 'high and fast' cooking technique at temperatures of 150°C-200°C/300°F-400°F, typically using gas and charcoal, uncovered (without a lid on the barbecue). This method is perfect for a quick bite to eat after work, when you don't have 6 hours to create some perfect ribs. Smaller, thinner and more tender types of cuts, such as steaks, burgers, chicken breasts and pork chops, and fish fillets and shellfish, work well using this direct method of cooking with live fire. When grilling, we prefer to use charcoal. It's your culinary rite to build a fire, so take the time to go coal. Plus you'll get better results, although flame control can be tricky.

We recommend a large charcoal kettle grill with a lid, such as the ones manufactured by Weber. If you prefer gas, then buy one that has more than 2 burners. That way you'll have the flexibility to use the gas grill for indirect cooking, too.

WHAT EXACTLY IS SMOKING (TRUE BARBECUE)?

This technique uses a 'low and slow' cooking method, smoking indirectly, near a low fire or in a pit at temperatures between 80-140°C/180-275°F,

using hardwood or charcoal (and sometimes gas). This style of barbecuing imparts smoke into large or tougher cuts of meat such as brisket, pork shoulder and ribs and can take all day or night, depending on the size of the product you are smoking (this means you may drink more beer when smoking versus grilling). As the meat basks in the low, smoky heat, the tough connective tissue in the meat, called collagen, starts to dissolve. As smoke permeates the outside of the meat, it often leaves a pink smoke ring about 1-2cm thick. We call this the Circle of Truth, and it's the sign that your meat has been barbecued in the traditional way.

To be a true barbecuer, you'll need to use either a kettle grill with lid and vents, a bullet smoker or an offset smoker. Using a gas grill for indirect cooking has its limitations, and it's not our favoured method, but to cover all set-ups we have included some tips on this equipment, too (see page 238).

AFTERBURN AND RESTING

The 'afterburn' effect on larger chunks of meat means that cooking continues after the meat has been removed from the heat, so don't be afraid to take the meat off the grill some time before it is cooked to your liking. It's super-important to let meat rest after cooking.

TO THE DETAILS

As meat is cooked, the proteins heat up and 'set'. The more cooked, the more set the proteins will be, and this is why we can judge how well done a piece of meat is simply by prodding it with tongs: the firmer the meat, the more 'done' it is. When the proteins set, they push the meat's juices towards the centre. Leaving the meat to rest away from the heat before serving allows the juices, which have been driven to the centre of the meat, to redistribute throughout and be reabsorbed. As a result, the meat will 'bleed' less when you cut it and be far more tender and juicy to eat.

MOPPING VS GLAZING

Mopping sauces, or mops, are used for imparting moisture and flavour into hunks of meat that are smoked low and slow for long periods of time. They are usually made of a mixture of vinegar and other tasty liquids like stock or beer and laced with seasonings and spices. They tend to be thin in consistency and never contain sugar, as the sugar will burn if subjected to heat for the duration of the smoking process.

Glazes do contain sugar and are usually thick in consistency, much like the ever-popular BBQ sauce we all know and love. Glazing only ever happens towards the end of the smoking or grilling process to give a sticky, caramelised flavour. Be careful not to burn your glaze, because it will spoil all your hard work and result in bitter-tasting meat.

SOAKING WOOD CHUNKS

There is a school of thought that says don't bother soaking your wood chunks or chips. We disagree. Soaking smaller pieces of wood before smoking helps to prevent them from flaming up immediately which can burn off any smoke, the very thing you want to pressure when smoking foods. Soaking helps to smoulder the wood instead. We do agree that soaking large logs is a waste of time. That is all.

STERILISING

Wash the jars or containers in hot water and dish soap thoroughly. Place the jars and lids in a large stock pot facing upwards, then fill with hot water. Bring the water to a full, rolling boil for 10 minutes. Using tongs, lift the jars, empty the hot water out of them and place them, open end up, on a paper towel for one minute to dry. Lift the lids out and place on the paper towel too. Be careful not to let the sterilised equipment touch anything except the clean paper towel.

While the jars are still hot, fill them with warm ingredients - adding hot ingredients to a cool jar may cause the jar to crack. Then seal the jars.

CHAPTER

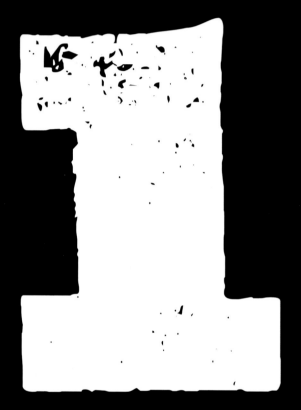

RUBS AND CRUSTS

RUBS

A rub is a mixture of herbs and spices used to flavour meat, fish and vegetables and can be as simple as massaging salt and pepper into a piece of meat before cooking. Rubs in smokehouse barbecue are a key factor in helping to form that essential outer crust of the meat with the salty, sweet, smoky and crunchy caramelised finish that's unique to low and slow barbecue.

The key to great barbecue rubs is the ratio of sugar (typically dark brown) to other ingredients. Some contain more sugar, others more salt. Sugar has a tendency to burn, even at relatively low temperatures, so when cooking for longer periods, make sure you use a rub that contains less sugar. We consider a long (or 'slow') cooking period to be 5 hours or more. Shorter (or 'faster') smoking periods range from 1 to 5 hours. Apply the dry rub into wet meat, using one dry hand to sprinkle the rub and the otherwet hand to massage the rub into all the crevices of the meat.

BASIC DRY RUB

This is our basic dry barbecue rub. The quantity might seem generous, but the mixture keeps well and lasts for 3 months if stored correctly. It's also the basis for some of the other rubs in this book: all you need to do is add spices to adapt it for other recipes.

MAKES 800G

250g soft dark brown sugar

125g caster sugar

125g smoked hot paprika

125g fine sea salt

50g cracked black peppercorns

25g ground ginger

50g garlic powder

25g ground cumin

25g cayenne pepper

1 Spread the brown sugar evenly over a baking sheet and leave it to dry in a cool, dark place for a few hours or overnight. This will help stop the rub clumping while in storage.

2 When the sugar has dried out, put it in a large bowl with the rest of the ingredients. Mix everything together well, breaking up any clumps of sugar with your fingers.

3 Place the rub mixture in a large airtight container and seal securely with a lid. Kept in a cool, dark place, the mixture will remain fresh for up to 3 months. After that, the spices start to lose their flavour.

SLOW PORK RUB

A 'slow' rub contains less sugar than its faster cousins, so it's more suitable for the longer cooking times required by larger primal cuts, such as pork shoulder. If your rub contains too much sugar, there is a danger it will burn and leave behind a bitter aftertaste in your pulled pork.

MAKES 650G

500g Basic Dry Rub
(see opposite)

100g fine sea salt

50g sweet paprika

1 tsp onion powder

1 tsp ground coriander

1 tsp ground fennel seed

1 Combine all the ingredients in a bowl. Mix well, making sure that you break up any clumps.

2 Store in an airtight container in a cool, dark place. This keeps for up to 3 months.

FAST PORK RUB

This rub contains a higher sugar to salt ratio and is intended for use with smaller pork cuts such as Smoked Baby Back Ribs (see page 26) or St Louis Cut (SLC) Ribs (see page 32).

MAKES 550G

500g Basic Dry Rub
(see opposite)

1 tsp onion powder

1 tsp mild chilli powder

½ tsp dried oregano

½ tsp dried sage

½ tsp dried marjoram

½ tsp dried parsley

½ tsp ground white pepper

1 Combine all the ingredients in a bowl. Mix well, making sure that you break up any clumps.

2 Store in an airtight container in a cool, dark place. This keeps for up to 3 months.

BEEF COFFEE RUB

We first experienced coffee and BBQ at Franklin Barbecue in Austin, Texas. They serve an amazing espresso-based BBQ table sauce that works really well with smoked beef. We figured that adding it as a rub to brisket at the beginning of the long smoke might be a worthwhile exercise.

MAKES 750G

200g Basic Dry Rub
(see opposite)

100g instant coffee granules

200g whole black
peppercorns, cracked

200g flaked sea salt

50g hot chilli or chipotle
powder

1 Combine all the ingredients in a bowl. Mix well, making sure that you break up any clumps.

2 Store in an airtight container in a cool, dark place. This keeps for up to 3 months.

BAY POULTRY RUB

This rub was developed by our pit masters in Leeds and really enhances the smoke profile while crisping up the skin of the chicken.

MAKES ENOUGH FOR 1 CHICKEN

2 whole dried bay leaves, or ½ tsp ground bay leaves

1 tbsp freshly ground black pepper

½ tbsp sweet paprika

1 tsp flaked sea salt

1 tsp garlic powder

½ tbsp soft light brown sugar

½ tsp ground cumin

1 If using whole bay leaves, add them to a pestle and mortar and pound into small, fine pieces.

2 Add the pounded bay leaves (or ground bay) to a mixing bowl along with the remaining ingredients. Mix together well, using your fingers to break up any lumps in the sugar.

3 This quantity is enough for 1 chicken but you can make a larger batch and store it in an airtight container in a cool, dark place for up to 1 month.

CABRITO DRY RUB

This simple dry rub is our take on a style of fajita that's used in southern Texas and Mexico on roast kid (goat), which yields incredibly tender meat. The animal carcass is butterflied and the mix rubbed all over it. Then the carcass is suspended over hot coals on a spike that is turned every 15-20 minutes. The resulting dish, Cabrito al-horno, provides the inspiration for this rub's name.

MAKES 300G, OR ENOUGH FOR A 13-15KG GOAT KID

60g cumin seeds

1½ tsp caraway seeds

1 tbsp dried rosemary

1 tbsp freshly ground black pepper

1 tbsp ground coriander

¼ tsp cayenne pepper

1 tbsp yellow mustard seeds

120g caster sugar

60g flaked sea salt

1 tbsp garlic powder

1 tbsp onion powder

1 Using a pestle and mortar, pound together the cumin seeds, caraway seeds and dried rosemary.

2 Place the pounded mixture and all the remaining ingredients in a large bowl and mix together well.

3 Apply generously to the meat, rubbing it all over the surface and into the crevasses with your fingers. Add more during the cooking process, if you like. The sugars will caramelise and help the other herbs and spices adhere to the meat while cooking.

4 Store any remaining rub in an airtight container in a cool, dark place for up to 1 month.

OLD BAY-STYLE RUB

Once adorning the wreaths of Olympic champions, the humble bay leaf is a herb that thinks it's a spice. Bay's complex flavour contains hints of mint, thyme, some oregano and aspects of coriander and clove. When applied to meat, it brings out the warmth of other spices and adds a complex flavour profile of its own. This seasoning recipe can be used on almost any fish, shellfish or mollusc and works remarkably well rubbed on to BBQ chicken just before it is smoked.

MAKES 125G

15 large dried bay leaves

2 tsp black peppercorns

1 tsp cayenne pepper

¾ tsp whole cloves

2 tbsp celery salt

1 tbsp English mustard powder

1 tsp ground white pepper

1 tsp ground nutmeg

1 tsp ground ginger

1 tsp sweet paprika

1 Place the bay leaves, peppercorns, cayenne pepper and cloves in a dry frying pan over a medium heat and roast for 2-3 minutes or until you can smell the aromas - but don't let them burn.

2 Remove the pan from the heat and tip the spices onto a plate to cool. Once they have cooled, add them to a coffee or spice grinder and grind them down to a fine powder.

3 Add the remaining ingredients to the grinder and grind until completely mixed.

4 Store in an airtight container in a cool, dark place for up to 1 month.

SEASONING CRUSTS

'Crust' is the term we use for a customised salt seasoning that has been adapted for use at the end of the cooking phase. This is a great way to add a zip of crunchy flavour to your meats. Iodised salt tastes way too harsh for finishing dishes, but un-iodised sea salt has a much softer, delicate flavour. Couple this with fragrant herbs, roasted spices and an acidic kick, and you're golden! Roasting your spices before blending them gives maximum flavour, especially as these crusts don't go through a cooking cycle the way regular rubs do.

There are two ways to prepare a seasoning crust. One is mixed in a way more akin to a dry rub while the other goes through a wet stage first, followed by a drying stage either in an open oven, under the sun or in a smoker. Both crusts end up dry, but the latter style makes use of interesting liquids like citric acid, alcohol and vinegar.

BASIC CRUST

MAKES APPROXIMATELY 200G

125g flaked sea salt

60g sweet paprika

1 tsp celery seeds

1 tsp dried basil

1 tsp course ground black pepper

1 tsp cayenne pepper

1 tsp onion powder

1 tsp garlic powder

1 Mix all the ingredients together in a bowl then add the mixture to a dry frying pan over a medium heat.

2 Stir the crust for 4-5 minutes, or until the spices start to give off their fragrant aroma and begin to darken. Do not let them burn.

3 Remove the pan from the heat. Once the crust mixture has cooled, seal it in an airtight container and store in a cool, dark place for up to 1 month.

PICKLEBACK CRUST

Bourbon and pickled cucumbers (or dill pickles) are the perfect accompaniment to slow-smoked BBQ meats. Finish your pulled pork with this pickleback crust to pump up the flavour game.

MAKES APPROXIMATELY 300G

100g Pickled Cucumbers (see page 181) or dill pickles

250g crushed sea salt

1 tsp grated lime zest

2 tsp fresh lime juice

1 tsp granulated sugar

1 tbsp pickling vinegar

50ml bourbon, such as Wild Turkey

1 Preheat the oven to 150°C/Gas 2, or its lowest heat setting, and line two baking trays with baking parchment. Place the pickled cucumbers in a blender or food processor and blend until smooth.

2 Add the smooth pickle paste and the remaining ingredients to a bowl and stir well, then spoon the mixture on to the parchment-lined baking sheets, spreading it out as much as possible. The more you can spread it out, the faster it will dry.

3 Put the trays into the oven but leave the door ajar. Let the paste dehydrate for about 6-10 hours, giving it a stir every 2-3 hours. Once the mixture is a dry-salt texture, leave it to cool.

4 When the mixture has cooled, add it to a coffee grinder (or use a pestle and mortar) and grind it to a fine dust. Seal in an airtight container and store in a cool, dark place for up to 1 month.

SMOKED GARLIC AND HERB CRUST

You can use pretty much any herb you like to create this finisher, as long as the choice of herb matches the target. You will need a smoker for this recipe, so make this while you're smoking your brisket. Oak works well, but any wood you are already smoking with will be great.

MAKES APPROXIMATELY 300G

50g fresh tarragon or fresh rosemary

1 clove garlic

250g crushed sea salt

1 tsp grated lemon zest

100ml fresh lemon juice

1 tsp caster sugar

1 Line a baking tray with baking parchment and set it aside. Finely chop your chosen fresh herb and the garlic and place in a bowl. Add the rest of the ingredients and stir well.

2 Spoon the wet salty mixture on the prepared baking tray, and then spread it out as much as possible. The more you can spread it out, the faster it will dry.

3 Put the tray into the smoker and smoke uncovered for about 10 hours. Give it a stir every 2-3 hours. Once the mixture is a dry-salt texture, leave it to cool.

4 When the mixture has cooled, add it to a coffee grinder (or use a pestle and mortar) and grind it to a fine dust. Seal in an airtight container and store in a cool, dark place for up to 1 month.

CHAPTER

SMOKED BABY BACK RIBS

Pork ribs are a smokehouse staple and the baby back cut (also known as loin ribs) is the most tender pork rib. True barbecue ribs should never fall off the bone - there should be a bite mark left behind when you chomp at them. For this recipe you need a charcoal grill with a lid, as you'll get the best results with this indirect way of cooking.

SERVES 4

4 slabs of baby back ribs, weighing 600–900g each, rinsed in cold water

4 tbsp yellow American mustard, such as French's

100g Basic Dry Rub
(see page 16), plus 50g
for finishing

100ml unsweetened apple juice

100ml cider vinegar

200g Kansas City BBQ Sauce
(see page 174), for glazing

WOOD

3–5 pieces of oak or cherry wood (our favourite for smoking pork ribs), or hickory, apple or mesquite if you want a deeper smoky flavour. Soak the wood before cooking with it.

1   Remove the back membrane from the ribs. This is not good to eat, as it becomes leathery. Set the ribs meaty-side down and, using a small round-ended knife, insert it along the end bone. Use a sheet of kitchen paper to help you grip the membrane, pull it away from the rack and discard it.

2   Slather each slab with 1 tablespoon of mustard then sprinkle with 25g of the dry rub, making sure to cover the ribs evenly on both sides. Wrap each slab in cling film and leave in the fridge to marinate for at least 4 hours (up to 12, if you like).

3   Prepare your smoker for a constant, indirect heat at 120°C (250°F) by pushing the coals aside and placing a foil tray of water below the ribs. This will catch any drips and create a moist environment for the ribs.

4   Thirty minutes before you are ready to cook them, take the ribs out of the fridge to allow them to reach room temperature. Remove the cling film and add a little more rub. Add 3 soaked wood chunks to the hot coals and leave them for 5 minutes to begin to smoulder before adding the ribs.

5   Place the ribs into the smoker on the top rack or shelf, meat-side up. If you are pushed for space, roll the ribs into coils, meat-side facing outwards, making sure there is enough space between each rack for the smoke to lick the inside of the coil. Close the lid of the smoker. While the meat is smoking, mix together the apple juice and cider vinegar in a clean, sterilised spray bottle (see page 13) to make a spritz.

6   After 1 hour, open the lid and, using long-handled tongs, take out the ribs and spray each rack on both sides with the spritz before returning them to the grill, meat-side up. Close the lid and add more wood chunks (and coal if needed, to maintain temperature).

CONTINUED

7 After 2 hours of smoking, prepare 4 sheets of double-layered aluminium foil. Remove the racks from the smoker and place one in the middle of each sheet. Before wrapping them in the foil, lift one side of the rack and spray each one 2-3 times with the spritz so the spritz pools between the foil and the meaty side of the ribs (this will help braise the ribs a little to encourage tenderness). Wrap them tightly in the foil to make a package known as a 'Texas Crutch'. Return the foil packages to the grill.

8 After 3 hours of smoking, remove the racks from the grill and take them out of the foil. Flip the ribs over and glaze both sides with BBQ sauce. Then put them back in the smoker, add the remaining chunks of wood and close the smoker.

9 After 30 minutes, glaze the ribs with the BBQ sauce on both sides again. At this point the ribs will be slightly bendy, which means they have tenderised. Grill for another 30 minutes then remove from the smoker. Sprinkle a little dry rub on the meaty side and leave to rest for 20 minutes, covered. Once rested, slice and serve.

COUNTRY-STYLE RIBS

The first thing to note about these ribs is that they are very meaty indeed. Their name was coined from old techniques witnessed out in the countryside, when butchers used handsaws and axes to butcher hog's ribs.

There are two variations of country rib. The first is not a true country rib, but is actually the offcut of a regular pork butt or Boston butt (the American name for the upper part of the shoulder of the front leg of the pig), where the shoulder has been squared off to get the classic shape, resulting in some good steaks. The flavour is much the same as a pork steak and has a good fat-to-meat ratio. It's smoked much the same way as you would a pork butt. However, a true country rib comes from the tail end of the loin and has a rib bone attached. It looks very much like a pork chop, but has a flavour profile similar to baby back ribs.

THIS THREE-STAGE RECIPE INVOLVES *smoking, braising and grilling.*

SERVES 6

6 tbsp Basic Dry Rub (see page 16)

6 x 225g country ribs

250ml unsweetened pineapple juice

500g Kansas City BBQ Sauce (see page 174), or South Carolina

WOOD

2 chunks of good fruitwood, soaked overnight or for at least 2 hours

1 Set your smoker for indirect cooking at 140°C (275°F) for 3 hours. Put the dry rub into a very large bowl. Add the ribs and toss them in the rub to get a good coating then leave them to marinate in the bowl, loosely covered with cling film, for 1 hour while you get the smoker up to temperature.

2 After 1 hour, place the ribs directly on the rack in the smoker, leaving enough space between each of them to get a good smoke-licking. Add the wood chunks and close the lid. Leave the ribs to smoke for 1 hour.

3 Pour the pineapple juice and BBQ sauce into a foil tray, or any other ovenproof roasting dish or casserole that you don't mind putting into your smoker, and mix them up well with a whisk. The pineapple juice will help to break down the fats and collagen in the meats and will thin out the BBQ sauce enough to keep it liquid.

4 After the ribs have had 1 hour in the smoker, check the internal temperature of the ribs using a digital probe thermometer. If they have reached 65°C (150°F), remove them from the smoker and put them in the BBQ sauce in the foil tray. Flip them over a few times, so they all get a good covering. Place a lid on the foil tray, with the foil side of the lid facing inwards and then seal them by folding over the edges. If the foil tray does not have a lid, or you are using an ovenproof dish, just seal it tightly with aluminium foil. We prefer using a double layer, which you first lay out on a clean work surface. This gives added durability, and prevents any holes or tears happening during handling.

CONTINUED

5 Return the foil tray to the smoker, which still needs to be at 140°C (275°F), and continue to cook for a further 1-1½ hours, or until the internal temperature of a rib in the centre of the foil tray reaches 90°C (195°F). Don't be worried about piercing straight through the lid into a rib to get your reading at this stage. The foil or the lid will have done their job of steaming the smoked ribs to perfection by now.

6 Once the ribs have reached the correct internal temperature, remove them from the braising liquor, and place them on a tray or plate. Return the uncovered foil tray to the smoker, until the liquid reduces by half. This will be used to glaze the ribs.

7 Remove the foil tray with the reduced BBQ liquid, and then put the ribs back into the smoker, which will still need to be at a high temperature of 140°C (275°F).

8 Use a brush to glaze the exposed side of the ribs, place the lid back on the smoker, and leave them to cook for 5 minutes. Open the smoker and flip all the ribs over. There should be a good glaze on the ribs now, and they should be hot and sizzling. Brush the remaining sides of the ribs, and put the lid back on, but only for 2-3 minutes this time, because the ribs should be real hot by now. Take out the ribs and serve.

ST. LOUIS CUT (SLC) RIBS

If you want a more impressive looking, meatier rack of ribs than baby backs, then pork spare ribs are a must. Baby backs lie near the spine. Spare ribs are attached to them and run all the way down to the chest. St. Louis cut ribs are spare ribs that have had the rib tips (the gristly featherbones you find along one length of the rack) removed.

SERVES 4

2 slabs spare ribs, weighing about 1.2kg each, rinsed under cold water

4 tsp fine sea salt

60g yellow American mustard, such as French's

90g Fast Pork Rub (see page 17), mixed with 40g cracked black peppercorns

100ml unsweetened apple juice

100ml cider vinegar

WOOD

4 chunks of apple or oak wood, soaked overnight or at least 2 hours

1 To skin and trim the spare ribs, set the ribs meaty-side down and, using a small round-ended knife, such as a butter knife, insert it along the end bone. Use a sheet of kitchen paper to help you grip the membrane, pull it away from the rack and discard it. Once you have skinned the ribs, trim any unwanted fat from the meaty side but be careful not to trim them too much. A little bit of fat will help keep the ribs moist throughout the long cooking process.

2 To separate the rib tips from the rack, you'll need a sharp knife. It's quite easy, and takes only two simple cuts. First, with the meat-side down and bone-side up, locate the flap of meat towards the narrow end of the rack. Slice the last bone (usually around 14 bones from the larger end) and flap of meat off to square the rack at the end. This flap will dry out during cooking, so is best removed early on.

3 The next step is to make a horizontal cut to separate the breastbone and cartilage. To find the sweet spot for this cut, first locate the longest rib, usually the fourth bone in on the wider end of the rack. Feel along that rib until you detect a softer spot. That's a cartilaginous section where the rib connects to the sternum (breastbone). Make the cut by inserting the knife into the soft spot, then slicing perpendicular to the ribs, cutting through all of the soft spots where each rib meets the breastbone. Once the breastbone has been removed, you should have a clean, rectangular rack of ribs with nothing but bone and meat. Keep the breastbone trimmings aside. These will now be called 'rib tips', and we'll be smoking them, too.

4 Dry-brine the St. Louis cut racks by lightly sprinkling 1 teaspoon of salt on each rack across each side. Wrap in cling film and refrigerate for 1-2 hours, to allow the salt to be absorbed.

5 Unwrap the racks and slather each slab with mustard and 2 tablespoons (50g) of the rub mixed with black pepper, making sure to cover them evenly on both sides (reserve the unused rub for later). As the ribs have already been dry-brined, there is no need to let the ribs marinate with the rub. Once the ribs are at room temperature (which should only take 1 hour out of the fridge) they're ready to go on the grill.

6 Prepare your smoker for indirect cooking at around 110°C (225°F). Add 3 pieces of the soaked wood to the hot coals and leave them to smoulder for a few minutes before adding the ribs.

CONTINUED

7 Place the ribs on the grill meat-side up. If you are pushed for space, you can use a rib rack to increase capacity. However, you'll need to add an extra hour of initial smoking to ensure the ribs are cooked to full tenderness. Close the lid of the smoker and leave to smoke for the first 3 hours. Mix together the apple juice and vinegar in a clean and sterilised spray bottle to make a spritz. Spray the meat once an hour while it is in the smoker.

8 After 3 hours, prepare two double-layered aluminium foil sheets. Remove the ribs from the smoker and place one rack in the middle of each sheet, meat-side down. Before wrapping, lift one side of a rack and spray it 2-3 times so the spritz pools between the foil and the meaty side of the ribs. Repeat with the other rack. This step will help braise the ribs a little to encourage tenderness. Now wrap them tightly in the foil and set them back on the grill for another 2 hours. Remember to top up your coal to maintain temperature.

9 After 2 hours, remove the racks from the foil, place them on a baking sheet and discard the foil and the juices. This is a good time to carry out the 'bend test' on the racks to check for 'doneness'. To do this, pick up each slab holding the first 3 bones with a pair of tongs and bounce them slightly. If they are ready, the slab will bow until the meat starts to crack on the surface. A small crack means you need a little more time. Fully cooked ribs should be close to breaking off when you lift the slab. You'll get the feel for this with practice, but at this stage you should still need another hour on the grill to fully tenderise the meat.

10 Some of the rub may have come away from the ribs by this stage due to the crutching phase so, using the tongs to flip the ribs, sprinkle the remaining rub back on both sides of the slabs. Add the remaining chunks of soaked wood to the pit and put the racks back on the grill for the final hour.

11 After this time, carry out another bend test. At this point the ribs should crack fully. Spray the ribs with the spritz and set them aside to rest for 20 minutes, covered loosely with foil. Once rested, slice and serve. If you've done all this right, you will notice that there is a thin pink layer beneath the surface of the meat. This does not mean it is undercooked! It is the highly prized smoke ring ('Circle of Truth', as we like to call it), caused by true low and slow smoking.

RIB TIPS

When a full-size slab of spare ribs is trimmed to a St. Louis cut rack, you are left with rib tips around 15cm long and 2.5cm thick. These fatty, cartilaginous offcuts are best over-smoked so the featherbones turn to jelly inside and the bark develops a crunchy, salty exterior, making them the perfect match for an icy cold beer or glass of chilled white wine.

SERVES 2

50g Fast Pork Rub (see page 17)

3 trimmed rib tips

100g Kansas City BBQ Sauce (see page 174), or your favourite ready-made sauce

3 tbsp smooth apricot jam

1 tsp soft dark brown sugar

1 Prepare your grill for indirect heat at around 120°C (250°F). Generously apply the pork rub to the rib tips, patting them gently so the rub adheres. Place the rib tips in your smoker for 3 hours, or until the ribs can be pulled apart with two forks.

2 Meanwhile, mix the BBQ sauce with the jam and the brown sugar in a small bowl. Remove the ribs tips from the grill and paint them generously with the sauce.

3 Place the rib tips back on the smoker and cook for a further 15 minutes. Remove the rib tips from the grill, cut and serve.

OUR AWARD WINNING PULLED PORK

Pulled pork is a good way to get into low and slow cooking. It is important to have a high-quality piece of meat, a great rub, enough time and to keep your smoker at a low and constant temperature. Sourcing a true pork shoulder or butt (aka Boston butt) can be tricky. A pork butt is square in appearance, and it still has the shoulder blade bone. This not only helps to conduct heat, but also keeps the meat from falling apart.

Smoking pork butt takes time; you'll notice that the temperature rises quite quickly at first, then after 6 hours or so remains the same, but once this stage has passed, the temperature will gradually increase, and the fats and collagens will start to melt, replacing all the moisture that was forced out during the stall. You can expect to lose up to 30 per cent of the original raw weight of the butt, so bear this in mind when you're cooking for a large group. Typically, you will need about 200g of cooked pulled pork per person.

SERVES 12-15

1 pork shoulder (pork butt)
with blade bone in, about 5kg

5 tsp salt

30ml vegetable oil or 30g yellow
American mustard, such as French's

100g Slow Pork Rub (see page 17),
plus 100g for seasoning the pulled pork

500ml unsweetened apple juice

250ml cider vinegar

250ml Kansas City BBQ Sauce
(see page 174)

1 The day before you plan to smoke the meat, remove the fat cap from the joint and then trim off most of the fat. You want the rub to flavour the meat and not the fat, and you also stand a better chance of getting that crunchy, flavoursome bark that flecks through the finished pulled pork. Check out our recipe for Cracklings (see page 194), and don't throw that fat cap in the bin.

2 Wash the whole joint under cold running water and dry it thoroughly. For each kg of raw pork, use 1 teaspoon of salt, and rub this all over the trimmed butt. Wrap the salt-rubbed meat in cling film and put it in the fridge overnight.

3 On the day of the smoke, rub the butt with the oil or the mustard, making sure to massage it in. Either of these will help to dissolve the rub ingredients and create the first layer of that all-important bark. Apply the rub evenly over the whole surface of the pork shoulder. Lift up any flaps of meat and get right into all the crevices. Set your smoker for indirect smoking at 110°C (225°F).

4 Set the pork on a rack (never directly on a tray or roasting pan) and place it in the preheated smoker so the smoke can penetrate the whole joint and the rendered fats can drip out of the butt.

CONTINUED

Pulled pork freezes and reheats really well. Place it in an ovenproof dish, cover and reheat slowly in the oven, or simply portion up any leftovers into microwaveable containers, and reheat on full power for 2–3 minutes, stirring halfway through the process.

5 Now mix the apple juice and cider vinegar in a clean, sterilised spray bottle to make a spritz. A butt of this size will take 12-16 hours to smoke, so it's important to monitor and maintain a constant temperature at all times. Spray the butt every hour or so with the spritz to enhance the bark and help the smoke flavour adhere better.

6 To get the perfect 'doneness' for pulled pork, the internal temperature of the pork must hit 95°C (200°F). This is the temperature at which all the fats and collagen have been broken down, and when the meat will pull easily. A good test and sign that your butt is done is if you can pull the blade bone out without any effort. When the pork butt is ready, take it from the smoker and put it into a large turkey-roasting pan or some other large receptacle to be pulled.

7 Using two forks, slowly tear at the meat and pull it into strands. Don't over-pull the meat because the larger the pieces, the more fats will be in the meat, and the more succulent each mouthful will be. Now pour in the Kansas City BBQ Sauce, and stir gently to mix. Add the remaining rub and about 100ml of the spritz mixture and stir these in carefully, too.

8 Keep the pulled pork covered to retain moisture while preparing your sandwiches, if making. Never leave it boiling on the hob to keep warm. If you do this the meat will become stringy and all the fat will render. Instead, put it in an insulated container such as a cool box, and wrap it in kitchen paper. You should have more than enough pulled pork for about 15 generous sandwiches.

EPIC
PULLED PORK SANDWICH

We pride ourselves on our truly low and slow Pulled Pork. It has won many first prizes at BBQ competitions, so is it any wonder then that we sell these sandwiches in the thousands in our restaurants, at festivals and at our pop-up food stalls across the UK? The combination of smoky, sweet and spicy pulled pork and BBQ sauce, the sharp tanginess of our dressed slaw, all sitting pretty in a soft bun turns a sandwich into an Epic Sandwich. For best results, serve straight away while the pulled pork is still warm.

MAKES 15 SANDWICHES

15 x 13cm Brioche Buns or freshly baked soft white rolls about 13cm in diameter, sliced

150g North Carolina BBQ Sauce (see page 168)

3kg Pulled Pork (see page 36)

1.5kg Red's Slaw (see page 139)

20g Pickleback Crust (see page 23), (optional)

150g Kansas City BBQ Sauce (see page 174)

Pork cracklings, to garnish

1 Gently toast the buns over hot coals on your BBQ, or in the kitchen using a toaster or grill. Be careful not to burn them: a good char mark will add a level of flavour to the sandwich, but lightly toasted is what we are aiming for.

2 Arrange all the bun bottoms in three rows of five. Arrange the tops on a separate area of your work surface, in the same order as the bottoms, to ensure each bottom is matched with its correct top when assembling the sandwiches. You want to build them as quickly as possible so the buns don't go soggy.

3 Drizzle the BBQ sauce into the prepared pulled pork and mix well. This vinegar-based sauce helps to keep the pork moist while cutting through the fats in the meat.

4 Scoop up a portion of pulled pork using a large slotted spoon and squeeze the liquid out of the meat. Add the meat to the bottom half of a toasted bun. Using another slotted spoon, take a level spoonful of the slaw and gently squeeze it to remove any excess dressing. Place this on top of the pulled pork. Do this as quickly as possible because the cold slaw will cause the pork to cool.

5 Finish the sandwich by sprinkling ½ teaspoon of Pickleback Crust over each one, then top with a level tablespoon of Kansas City BBQ Sauce and a few pork cracklings.

6 Place the bun tops on sandwiches at a slant to reveal all the glorious fillings. Present on a serving platter, or plate individually if you prefer.

BACON BOMB

One cold winter's day, shortly after returning from a tiring pilgrimage, James D was hungry and a little bored. So, off he went, and after a few hours he returned with the Bacon Bomb.

SERVES 4-6

1 tbsp soft dark brown sugar

1 tbsp dried oregano

4 tsp sweet paprika

2 tsp garlic powder

1 tsp salt

1 tsp freshly ground black pepper

100g fresh breadcrumbs

300g steak mince

300g pork mince

2 medium onions, finely chopped

1 fresh green chilli, deseeded and diced

2 Texas Hotlinks (see page 91), (optional)

1 Bacon Weave (see page 136)

150g mild Cheddar cheese, grated

WOOD

2 chunks of oak or fruitwood, soaked overnight or for at least 2 hours

1 Set your smoker for indirect cooking at 190°C (375°F). Combine the sugar, oregano, paprika, garlic powder, salt, black pepper and breadcrumbs. In a separate, larger bowl, mix together the mince with the onion and green chilli.

2 Oil the sausages and gently fry them over a medium heat for about 5 minutes, or just long enough to crisp up the skin.

3 Mix the meat and rub together completely. Test the seasoning by frying up a small batch, taste and adjust the seasoning of the meat mixture accordingly.

4 Spread out a double layer of aluminium foil on a work surface and make the bacon weave (see page 136). Lay out a double layer of cling film the same size as the bacon weave. Take the mince, put it on top of the cling film and shape it to fit the same rectangle as the weave.

5 Put the grated cheese down the middle of the minced meat. Cut the ends off the sausages, so they marry up together when you put them on top of the cheese along the length of the mince.

6 Roll this into a larger sausage shape, encasing the cheese and sausages. Remember to make sure the sausage and meat filling is not longer than the bacon weave. Wrap in the cling film and place in the fridge for 1 hour to set.

7 Once set, remove the cling film and place the sausage into the centre of the bacon weave. Carefully wrap the sausage in the foiled bacon weave, and then tuck in the corners to keep in as much moisture as possible. Put the whole thing on a baking sheet, and place it into the hot smoker.

8 Cook for about 3 hours, or until the internal temperature reaches 71°C (160°F), remove the foil, add a chunk of wood to the coals for good measure, and smoke for a further 30 minutes to crisp up the bacon. Leave to rest for 5 minutes before cutting into portions.

MAKE YOUR OWN...
BACON

HOME-SMOKED MAPLE BACON

Ask your butcher for fresh pork belly, which lies on top of the spare ribs, and is called 'side bacon' or 'streaky bacon'. There are two ways of curing bacon at home: dry curing and wet curing. This old-fashioned recipe calls for Prague Powder #1, which is usually a pink coloured curing salt, it's 6 per cent sodium nitrite and 94 per cent table salt. Prague Powder #1 is available online. It's really important to keep to the salt-cure ratios in the recipe below. If your pork belly weighs more or less, adjust the quantities accordingly.

MAKES APPROXIMATELY 1.6KG

2 tbsp fine sea salt

2 tsp Prague Powder #1 curing salt

2 tbsp coarse ground black pepper

4 tbsp soft dark brown sugar

4 tbsp Basic Dry Rub (see page 16)

270ml maple syrup or honey

350ml water

2kg whole fresh pork belly (bottom end, streaky), trimmed

WOOD

Apple or cherry wood chunks, soaked for at least 2 hours

1 In a large bowl, mix together the salts, pepper, sugar, dry rub, maple syrup (or honey) and the water. Mix well to dissolve the ingredients.

2 Cut the pork belly into quarters. Ladle four equal parts of the curing liquid into four sturdy Ziplock bags, then add a pork belly quarter to each. Remove as much air from the bags as possible and zip them shut. Mix the meat and the curing liquid together really well, pushing the spices into the meat without breaking the plastic.

3 Once you have done this with all four bags, put them into a container to catch any leaks. Place the meat in the fridge at about 1-3°C (34-37°F) for 7 days. Each day, massage each bag so the juices and spices are evenly spread and flip over to the other side. If the pork belly is thicker than 3.5cm, leave to cure in the fridge for an additional 2 days.

4 Remove the cured bacon pieces from the fridge, discard the curing liquid, and wash them under cold running water so the surface isn't too salty. Pat the meat dry, but try not to remove the spices that may have clung to it.

5 Prepare your smoker for indirect cooking at 110°C (225°F) using the apple or cherry wood. Place the bacon in the smoker, and cook until they reach an internal temperature of 65°C (150°F). This should take 1-2 hours. Remove from the smoker, let them cool, and then refrigerate. Once cold, your bacon can be sliced. Slice on a slicer if you have one, or use a long, thin knife. Wrap the bacon tightly in several layers of cling film and refrigerate for up to 2 weeks. You can also slice all the bacon, layering the slices and separating individual portions with greaseproof paper, roll them up and wrap in cling film before freezing for up to 3 months.

BEEF BACON

Like pork bacon, beef bacon is simple to make. While it's a healthier alternative to pork bacon, being about 90 per cent lean, it is a little drier than its pork cousin.

MAKES ABOUT 800G

1kg piece of short rib beef, bones removed, standing at least 4cm tall at its thickest end

Stage I
Dry cure rub

120g flaked sea salt

3 tbsp course ground black pepper

3 tbsp soft dark brown sugar

60g Red's Pickling Spice (see page 181)

1 tsp Prague Powder #1 curing salt

Stage II
Beef bacon smoke rub

2 tbsp Beef Coffee Rub (see page 17)

1 tbsp pure maple syrup

If your beef rib has really narrow ends that won't yield good slices of bacon, try slicing them as thinly as possible into strips, and dry them out in a low oven with the door slightly ajar: it's practically jerky.

1 Mix the ingredients for the dry rub in a bowl. Dry the beef rub meat with some kitchen paper to remove any excess juices. Generously apply two-thirds of the curing rub to the meat to coat.

2 Place half of the remaining rub in a dish large enough to hold the meat, then place the meat onto the rub, sprinkle and press the rest of the rub into the top and sides of the meat. Cover loosely with cling film and place in the fridge for 1 hour.

3 Remove the meat from the fridge and make sure it is uniformly flat, and that there are no areas doubling over. Wrap the meat tightly in cling film, then place into a Ziplock bag.

4 Place the sealed meat in the fridge in a bowl to catch any liquid, and leave it to cure for 5-7 days, depending on the thickness of the rib meat. If the rib meat is thicker than 5cm, then cure it for longer. On the day it is ready, remove the cured beef bacon from the Ziplock bag and cling film and thoroughly rinse the dry cure rub off of the meat under cold water. Pat the cured beef dry with kitchen paper. You will need to do this several times to get rid of all the rub. Set the meat aside while you set your smoker for indirect smoking at 93°C (199°F).

5 Rub the Stage II beef coffee rub all over the meat, getting an even coating all over. Drizzle over the maple syrup, and work it into the meat.

6 Place the rubbed cured beef bacon into your smoker, as well as chucking a good-sized wood chunk (oak or cherry) on the coals, and close the lid. The smoking time will be 3-4 hours, at 95°C (200°F).

7 Once the meat reaches an internal temperature of 65.5°C (150°F), remove it from the smoker and leave to cool for 30 minutes. Place it in the fridge, where it will need to cool down to 8°C so the fats in the bacon can set. It's best to leave it in the fridge overnight.

8 Slice the bacon across, into 5mm slices, with a very sharp carving knife. You will notice the meat is a ruby-pink red colour. This is due to the curing process, and potentially the smoke ring meeting in the middle. Wrap any leftover bacon tightly in cling film, and put it in the fridge for up to 10 days. You can also freeze beef bacon for up to 3 months.

TEXAS-STYLE SMOKED BEEF BRISKET

Before Red's opened we'd toiled over this recipe. After many years of trial and error, great successes and dismal disappointments, we're now happy to share our techniques to help pitmasters smoke the finest piece of beef they will ever experience.

A brisket is made up of two parts: the point (moist) is the part that sits on the top of the cut, and the flat (lean), is the bottom. The main difference is that the point has a load more fat content, and therefore requires longer cooking. The end that consists of mostly flat is also referred to as the hunk of flat (HOF), while the remaining part is known as the hunk of point (HOP). One thing to bear in mind is that the HOF will cook faster than the HOP so check those temperatures closely during the smoke. Remember: 'lookin' ain't cookin'', so be sure to invest in a remote digital probe. Ask your butcher to order in a whole untouched brisket, which is essentially the whole muscle taken straight from the beast. The untouched brisket will need to be trimmed of a lot of its fat. The aim is to remove excess fat while leaving behind a good 1cm layer. This is essential for keeping your brisket moist and tender after the smoke.

HOF or HOP brisket, weighing 5–7kg, trimmed

25ml olive oil, plus extra for rubbing

100g Beef Coffee Rub (see page 17)

100ml Worcestershire sauce

100ml water

WOOD

About 4 decent-sized chunks of air-dried oak for 3 hours' smoking, plus extra if needed. All soaked in water overnight or for at least 2 hours.

1 The day before you want to smoke, prepare the brisket. Trim the fat off the underside of the brisket (not the point side) to enable the rub to penetrate the meat and give a better flavour.

2 Rub the trimmed brisket with olive oil and then the beef coffee rub. Make sure you work it in well. We use oil mostly because spices are more soluble in oils than they are in water-based substances like mustard, which is also a popular ingredient, added in the rub stage. And remember to RUB, not sprinkle! Wrap the rubbed beef in cling film and place in the fridge to marinate for at least 24 hours. The salt in the rub will help to give the brisket a good smoke ring, whilst all the sugars and spices will dissolve and their flavours will start to penetrate the meat.

3 Take the brisket out of the fridge a couple of hours before it goes in the smoker to allow it to reach room temperature. Meanwhile, prepare your smoker for indirect cooking at 150°C (300°F).

4 When the smoker is ready, place the beef inside, point-side down. This is important as the fat will insulate the meat and keep it moist. Insert a digital probe thermometer into the thickest part of the brisket. Add a couple of chunks of wood (remember to keep checking these do not burn out) and keep them topped up for the first 3 hours. Smoke the brisket for 3 hours at 150°C (300°F).

5 Roll out enough aluminium foil (shiny-side up) to wrap the brisket. Drizzle the foil with the olive oil, and then rub it all over the surface of the foil. The oil helps to dilute the spices, and improves the punchiness of the rub.

6 Place the meat in the smoker. Meanwhile, mix the Worcestershire sauce and water together in a clean, sterilised spray bottle to make a spritz. Once the meat reaches an internal temperature of 60°C (140°F), remove it from the smoker and place it HOP-side up on the oiled aluminium foil. Generously spray the whole piece of meat with the spritz, and give it another generous sprinkling of any leftover beef rub for added flavour if you like. Wrap the whole thing up in such a way that will create a sealed vessel. When you open it later you can collect all the lovely juices.

CONTINUED

7 Place the wrapped brisket in the smoker, being careful not to puncture the foil. The sealed foil package will speed the cooking process and ensure that the meat stays tender. This technique is known as crutching and its main objective is to help harness the heat already in the meat, and ensure a constant increase in temperature during the 'stall'.

8 Let the meat continue to smoke at 150°C (300°F) for a further 2 hours, or until it reaches an internal temperature of 80°C (176°F). At this point, open up your smoker and gently peel back enough of the foil from the top of the brisket to enable you to lift the meat out without losing the beefy juices in the bottom of the foil. Carefully pour all of the juices into a jug or bowl and reserve. Leave the brisket in the smoker for a further hour at 150°C (300°F) to help finish off the bark and ensure a good texture on the outside of the meat.

9 After 1 hour, or when the brisket reaches an internal temperature of 92°C (197°F), remove it from the smoker. Wrap the brisket in cling film, and then in an old towel or blanket and place it into a cool box.

10 Allow the brisket to rest undisturbed for at least 1 hour. When you are ready to serve the brisket, the way in which you cut it will be dictated by the result of your smoke. Rule of thumb is that you always cut against the grain. This gives a much more tender slice of meat because of the way the muscle strands lie in conjunction with your teeth chewing them. So for this reason if you've overdone it, slice it thin, but if it's just right, go ahead and slice off thick manly portions. This is straightforward when you have smoked a HOF. But in a perfectly smoked HOP, the grain of the flat and the point run in different directions. If you've smoked a HOP, it will have flat as part of it, so follow the instructions as above. Once you get to the point, you can do one of three things. 1: Separate the point muscle from the flat, and cut both pieces perpendicular to the grain of the meat. 2: Turn the whole piece 90 degrees and slice through both muscles. This will result in both muscles being cut through perpendicular at a 45-degree angle, resulting in a much more tender slice of brisket. 3: Remove the point, and return it to the smoker, and turn to page 52 and continue with our Burnt Ends recipe.

11 Serve the brisket immediately for best results, and preferably with the warmed up juices retained from the foil, with a touch of your favourite BBQ sauce whisked in for added flavour and moisture.

KANSAS CITY-STYLE BURNT ENDS

These nuggets of pure BBQ gold were not always held in such high esteem in the 'cue joints of old. Burnt Ends were mainly made up of the oddly shaped, drier, tougher offcuts of the pitmasters' briskets, as they sliced them for their punters. However the chunks of super-flavoured smoky bites soon became renowned in the Kansas City regions, where they were mixed with sweet, sticky sauce, and often put in sandwiches. Burnt Ends are an essential ingredient in our Pit Beans recipe (see page 154).

A proper Burnt End should always have at least one side boasting a good char or bark. It should be well cooked, and never spongy in texture, and here we demonstrate how to make these little cubes of gold, enabling you to get the most out of the money and time you've invested in your brisket. Please note that it is best to make Burnt Ends using a brisket that is still hot. If you want to cook a brisket entirely for the purpose of making Burnt Ends, please follow the method for smoking brisket, and then follow the recipe below.

SERVES 2-4

1kg smoked point from a brisket
(see page 48)

50g Beef Coffee Rub
(see page 17)

200g Kansas City BBQ Sauce
(see page 174)

200ml unsweetened
apple juice

1 Take the point that was removed from the brisket and return it to a smoker burning at 120°C (250°F) and place another chunk of air-dried oak on the coals. Leave the point to smoke for 2 hours.

2 When it reaches an internal temperature of 93°C (199°F), remove it from the smoker and place it on a chopping board. Leave it there to cool for 5-10 minutes, then cut it into 3cm cubes. Place the cubes in an ovenproof dish or roasting tin.

3 Add the beef coffee rub to the cubed meat and toss everything together to get an even distribution of rub on the meat. Add the BBQ sauce and the apple juice and give it a stir. (We add the apple juice to let down the sauce, so that when it reduces in the next stage of cooking you are left with a smooth, sweet sauce that is not too sticky or caramelised.)

4 Return the dish to the smoker, which should still be at 120°C (250°F). After 20 minutes, open up the smoker and toss the burnt ends in the sauce to get a good coating on each and every nugget. Leave the Burnt Ends to smoke for a further 40 minutes, or until the sauce has reduced by half. Serve up on their own as a real meat treat, or simply between two pieces of your favourite bread.

ᴛʜᴇ PITMASTER

Now we present the ultimate BBQ pit sandwich. It's called The Pitmaster because it showcases the very best of low and slow smoked meats in one incredible sandwich. Justin and Diane Fourton from Pecan Lodge, Dallas, make the most perfect example using old-school smoking techniques in their custom-built, oak-fired smoker, called Lurlene. On returning to the UK we had to give this sandwich a Red's twist and add it to this book, so you can all grab a taste of this outstanding 'cue joint's creation. Be sure to use the softest, freshest bun you can get your hands on. You're going to need to be able to get your jaws around this monster!

MAKES 1 SANDWICH

1 bread bun of your choice
(we use brioche or potato buns)

2 tsp Dirty Mayo (see page 77)

1 thick slice of smoked brisket
(see page 48)

100g Pulled Pork (see page 36)

1 home-made Jalapeño Cheddar
Link (see page 92), or your favourite
sausage

50g South Carolina BBQ Sauce
(see page 169), or prepared English
mustard

1 heaped tbsp Red's Slaw
(see page 139)

1 fresh green chilli (such as jalapeño),
thinly sliced into rounds, with seeds

2 Deep-fried Pickles (see page 193)

½ tsp Basic Crust (see page 16)

1 Slice the bun in half and toast it over an open fire or in a toaster. Smear a teaspoon of the mayo on to each toasted side of the bun. Fold the slice of brisket and add to the bottom half of the bun, and then top with the pulled pork.

2 Cut the sausage on an angle and set the slices on top of the pulled pork. Drench all the meats with the BBQ sauce or mustard. Next, add the slaw, and finish by crowning with 3-4 slices of green chilli and the fried pickles, seasoned with the basic crust. Place the bun top at an angle on the side of the sandwich, and present this masterpiece to your face.

BBQ SALT BEEF
AND BRAISED CABBAGE

Every March on St Paddy's Day, we honour our Irish customers with a twist to their classic corned beef and cabbage dish, the twist being the addition of a smoked bark finish and punchy liquor to loosen up the vegetables. Using curing salt helps the corned beef keep a nice pink colour.

SERVES 6

2kg rolled brisket (flat)

2 large onions, peeled and quartered

2 carrots, cut into thumb-sized chunks

2 medium green cabbages, quartered

6 medium potatoes, peeled and halved

3 tbsp roughly chopped fresh parsley

freshly ground black pepper, to taste

prepared horseradish from a jar, to taste

Brine

3 litres water

600g fine sea salt

600g soft light brown sugar

8 whole cloves

8 dried bay leaves

4 cloves garlic, crushed

4 star anise

5 sprigs fresh thyme

2 tsp Prague Powder #1 curing salt (optional)

Cooking liquor

50ml bourbon, such as Wild Turkey

1 tbsp Worcestershire sauce

4 cloves garlic, crushed

5 dried bay leaves

100g Kansas City BBQ Sauce (see page 174), or your favourite ready-made BBQ sauce

1 Combine the ingredients for the brine in a large saucepan and bring to the boil, stirring occasionally. Remove from the heat and leave to cool.

2 Place the brisket in a non-reactive container, pour in the brine and weigh the meat down with a clean stone or some plates so it is submerged under the brine. Cover the container and place in the fridge for 1 week, turning the meat every day.

3 After the week, discard the brine and place the meat in another, similar-sized container. Cover with fresh water, and leave in the fridge for a further 24 hours to remove some of the excess salt.

4 The following day, prepare your grill for indirect heat by pushing the coals to one side. Place the meat and vegetables in a pan large enough to accommodate both and that can be used on the grill. To make the cooking liquor, add the bourbon, Worcestershire sauce, garlic cloves and bay leaves to the saucepan and add water to cover. Place the pan directly over the coals, and let simmer for 2-3 hours, or until the meat is tender.

5 Remove the meat and place it on the indirect-heat section of the grill. Set the saucepan aside and smoke the brisket for 1½ hours. Add more wood chunks and coal to maintain a cooking temperature of 110°C (225°F).

6 Fifteen minutes before the end of the smoking time, place the saucepan (covered with a lid) back on the grill directly over the hot coals, and add another handful of coal to the grill. Cover the grill and continue smoking the brisket and liquor. After about 10 minutes, the liquor should be simmering. Add the vegetables to the saucepan and cover.

7 Once the brisket has been smoked for 1½ hours, remove the lid from the grill and brush the meat generously on both sides with BBQ sauce. After 20 minutes, or once the veggies are cooked, remove them from the saucepan using a slotted spoon and set aside to keep warm.

8 Place the saucepan containing just the cooking liquor over the hottest coals without the lid in place to reduce the liquor by half. This may take up to 30 minutes. Glaze the corned beef once more on both sides and replace the lid on the grill.

WOOD

About 4 decent-sized chunks of air-dried oak for 3 hours of smoking, plus extra if needed. All soaked in water overnight or at least 2 hours.

9 After 15 minutes, open the grill lid and set the corned beef aside to rest under loose aluminium foil. Continue reducing the liquor in the saucepan for a further 15 minutes. You can leave the grill lid off from now on.

10 Just before serving, place the veggies back in the liquor, cover and let them warm through. Slice the rested corned beef against the grain. Serve up the sliced corned beef and chunky veggies with the punchy liquor in a deep dish and top generously with chopped parsley, black pepper and prepared horseradish.

CLASSIC REUBEN SANDWICH

Our first Reuben experience was at Katz's Deli in New York in 2002 and, since then, we've spent many hours perfecting our own version of this classic hot sandwich. Russian dressing is better with chilli sauce than ketchup: we like the extra kick. Adding caraway seeds to the dressing gives an authentic Eastern European component, which is where, some say, US smokehouse barbecue originates.

MAKES 1 HUGE SANDWICH

3 slices rye bread

2 tbsp unsalted butter, softened

2 tbsp Russian dressing

6 thin slices BBQ Salt Beef
(see page 56)

2 tbsp Sauerkraut, drained
(see page 186)

¼ tsp caraway seeds (optional)

2 slices Swiss cheese

1 Pickled Cucumber
(see page 181)

freshly ground black pepper, to taste

Russian dressing

1 tbsp mayonnaise

1 tbsp Louisiana Hot Sauce
(see page 175), or ketchup

1 tsp jarred horseradish, drained

½ tsp finely chopped white onion

1 In a glass bowl, combine all the Russian dressing ingredients together and mix well with a metal spoon. Chill in the fridge for 30 minutes so all the flavours can hang out together and make friends.

2 Take the dressing out of the fridge. Butter one side of each slice of rye bread and set on a breadboard. Place all the remaining ingredients in front of you, including the Russian dressing, so you can build the sandwich.

3 Add ingredients in the following order to the buttered bread; 1 tablespoon of Russian dressing, spread evenly; 3 slices of corned beef; a twist of freshly ground pepper; 1 tablespoon sauerkraut with a light sprinkling of caraway seeds, if using; 1 slice Swiss cheese. Place another slice of bread on top and repeat the process. Crown the sandwich with the remaining slice of rye.

4 Preheat a frying pan over medium-high heat, and carefully place the sandwich in the pan. Heat the sandwich for approximately 3 minutes on each side, or until the bread is golden brown and the cheese has melted.

5 Slice the pickled cucumber in half, and secure it on top of the hot sandwich with a cocktail stick before serving.

NACHO PIE

We first came across this dish at Big D's BBQ competition in Dallas. It's a really clever way of serving up street food as a hand-held meal aka 'walking tacos'. You have to make sure the crisps packet you use is made of foil, as plastic packets will shrink when the hot food is placed inside. If you can't get Fritos or Doritos, other flavoured nacho-style chips will work, too. Alternatively, the whole pie could be made in a casserole and baked in the oven if served at the table.

SERVES 4

Brisket chilli

1 tbsp olive oil

2 cloves garlic, crushed

1 medium onion, finely diced

2 large dried ancho chillies, finely diced

1 tsp ground cumin

½ tsp ground coriander

400g smoked brisket cut into 1cm cubes, or Burnt Ends (see page 52) of a similar size

165ml Mexican beer

400g can chopped tomatoes

1 tbsp tomato purée

30g dark chocolate, chopped

340g can kidney beans, drained

4 packets of foil-pack nacho-style chips

Salsa

1 small onion, diced

1 fresh jalepeño pepper, diced

2 plum tomatoes

1 tbsp chopped fresh coriander

juice of ½ lime

salt and freshly ground black pepper

Garnish

200g mild Cheddar cheese, grated

200ml soured cream

1 fresh lime, quartered

1 Put the olive oil in a saucepan over a medium-high heat, add the garlic and onion. Cook for 2 minutes. Stir in the ancho chillies, cumin and ground coriander, and cook for a further 2 minutes.

2 Add the brisket or Burnt Ends and stir for 3 minutes to get some heat into the meat and help render some more of the fat.

3 Pour in the beer, chopped tomatoes and tomato purée and stir. Then throw in the dark chocolate. Increase the heat to high, and bring everything to the boil, before turning the heat back down to low.

4 Add the kidney beans. Give the chilli a good stir and let it simmer gently for about 2 hours.

5 While the chilli is cooking, make the salsa. Add the onion and jalapeño pepper to a small bowl and stir. Deseed the tomatoes by cutting them into wedges and running a knife along the flesh under the seeds to take them off. This leaves you with a petal-shaped piece of tomato. Dice this and add it to the bowl. Add the coriander and lime juice, season with salt and pepper to taste, stir well and set aside.

6 When you are ready to serve the Nacho Pie, take each packet of nachos and carefully cut along the long side of the packet to give it the widest opening. Shake the packet to shift all the chips closer together to the bottom, and set on a serving plate.

7 To serve, divide the brisket chilli between the four open packs. Now, while the chilli is piping hot, divide the grated cheese between each portion, so it melts a little. To finish, garnish each nacho pie with lashings of salsa and a big dollop of soured cream. Stick a fork in each packet and serve with a lime wedge for an extra citrus kick.

BRUNSWICK STEW

This is a great recipe for using up those leftover BBQ meats that might be kicking around in the fridge or freezer, and is a wonderful way to add punchy flavours to a meal on a winter's day. This is traditionally served with saltine crackers in the States, but would be perfectly good with some freshly baked, buttered bread such as Rye Sourdough (see page 149).

SERVES 6-8

100g pancetta, cut into small cubes, or smoked bacon lardons

1 tsp olive oil

1 green chilli, deseeded and sliced

500g skinless, boneless chicken thigh fillets, diced

750ml chicken stock

250g waxy potatoes, such as Charlotte, Maris Peer, or Jersey Royals, peeled and cut into 1cm cubes

1 large carrot, finely diced

1 stick celery, finely diced

1 dried bay leaf

200g Pulled Pork (see page 36)

100g canned or frozen sweetcorn

400g can cannellini beans, drained

1 medium onion, finely diced

340g can chopped tomatoes

1 tbsp red wine vinegar

juice of ½ lemon

salt and freshly ground black pepper

dash of Louisiana Hot Sauce (see page 175) or your favourite shop-bought one

1 Fry the pancetta or bacon in the oil in a saucepan over a medium-high heat until crisp and golden. Remove from the pan and set aside. Now throw in the chilli, roast it in the pan for 1 minute, and then add it to the bacon.

2 Season the chicken with salt and pepper, brown it in the same pan for 2-3 minutes and add to the bacon and chilli.

3 Now take about one-third of the chicken stock and use it to deglaze the bottom of the pan. Using a wooden spoon, stir and dislodge all of the sticky bits on the bottom and sides of the pan into the stock. Carry on cooking until the liquid has reduced by half.

4 Add the potatoes, carrot and celery, and stir them in the stock for 2 minutes to get some heat and flavour into them. Return the bacon, chicken and chilli to the pan along with the remaining chicken stock and the bay leaf. Bring everything to a fast simmer, and then turn the heat down real low.

5 Let the stew cook for 1 hour, but give it a stir every 15 minutes or so to make sure it's just ticking over. Add the pulled pork, and leave the mixture to simmer for another 30 minutes. Then add the sweetcorn, beans, onion and chopped tomatoes. Continue to simmer for a further 30 minutes, or until the stew has thickened.

6 To bring the whole dish to life, add the red wine vinegar, lemon juice and hot sauce just before serving and give it all a good stir.

LOW AND SLOW SMOKED BBQ BEEF LONG WITH RASPBERRY CHIPOTLE BBQ SAUCE

This is the stuff of legends, and if you've never had a smoked beef rib, get it on your bucket list. It might be a challenge finding such ribs in your local supermarkets, so talk to your butchers. Ask for a Jacob's Ladder (also called short rib), which will have 6-8 bones of about 25-30cm in length on each rack. The layer of meat will be 2.5-5cm thick from one end to the other.

SERVES 6

1 rack Jacob's ladder (about 4kg)

1 tbsp olive oil

30g Beef Coffee Rub (see page 17)

100ml water

100ml Worcestershire sauce

Raspberry Chipotle
BBQ Sauce

30g unsalted butter

2 small shallots, finely diced

1 clove garlic, crushed

100g soft light brown sugar

juice of 1 orange, plus grated zest
of ½ orange

½ tsp salt

½ tsp ground ginger

½ tsp freshly ground black pepper

3 whole cloves

500ml Judas Ketchup (see page 173)
or your favourite shop-bought ketchup

125g seedless raspberry jam

40g Chipotles in Adobo (see page 178),
puréed

1 The night before you want to cook the dish, oil the whole rack and sprinkle the rub over the top of the Jacob's ladder. There is no need to rub the bones because the rack is cooked meat-side up, but be sure to work a good layer of rub into the sides to create a good bark. Wrap in cling film and leave in the fridge overnight to marinate.

2 The next day, remove the cling film and return to room temperature. Once the ribs are ready to be smoked, set your smoker for indirect cooking at 110°C (225°F). When the smoker is ready, place the ribs inside, bone-side down. Put some chunks of wood on the coals, and close the lid. Mix together the water and Worcestershire sauce in a clean, sterilised spray bottle to make a spritz and set aside.

3 Beef ribs need a long smoke to enable the internal temperature to get high enough to break down all the fats and collagen which, when melted, replace the water content in the meat and gives it that all-important wobble that tells you it has cooked to perfection. To achieve this the meat needs an internal temperature of 95°C (200°F). A rough guide is that a layer of meat 2.5cm thick will take up to 7 hours to smoke, while a 5cm layer will take up to 10 hours. There is no need at all to crutch beef ribs (i.e. wrap them in foil to accelerate the cooking process). If you do this you will be left with braised beef, not low and slow smoked beef.

CONTINUED

WOOD

About 4 decent-sized chunks of air-dried fruit wood or oak, all soaked in water overnight or for at least 2 hours

4 While the ribs are smoking, make the Raspberry Chipotle BBQ Sauce (see page 64). Melt the butter in a saucepan over a low heat. Add the shallots and garlic and gently fry until they have softened. Add the sugar, the orange juice and zest, salt and the spices, and cook for about 2 minutes, or until the sugar has dissolved. Add the ketchup, the jam and finally the chipotle purée. Stir well until everything is blended. Reduce the heat to low and simmer the sauce for 30 minutes. Remove from the heat, leave to cool slightly, then decant it into a sterilised jar or bottle with a lid (see page 13). Seal and refrigerate until the final hour of the smoke. Any leftover sauce will keep in the fridge for 1 month.

5 During the long cooking time for the ribs, maintain a constant temperature, and keep an eye on the thinner bones. If necessary, move the Jacob's ladder to cooler spots in your smoker to protect those vulnerable and valuable bones. Every hour or so, spray the Jacob's ladder with a little of the spritz to enhance the smoke flavour and improve the bark. When the beef ribs are about 1 hour away from being well and truly smoked to perfection, brush the whole rack with a layer of the Raspberry Chipotle BBQ Sauce to glaze the meat for the final hour of the smoke.

MAKE YOUR OWN...
JERKY

BEEF JERKY

Drying meat into travel food has been one of the great constants of humanity. Some unknown prehistoric person discovered that drying meat, especially with salt and spices, creates a food that will last through the lean months. Folks have been chewing on it ever since. Before you can make jerky, you'll need to knock up a drying cabinet or dehydrator (see page 242), or you can buy one.

MAKES 3KG

5kg lean beef silverside

500g flaked sea salt, crushed

400ml brown malt vinegar

200ml Worcestershire sauce

100ml bourbon

50g garlic powder

500g black peppercorns, cracked

500g coriander seeds, toasted and cracked

100g dried chilli flakes

1 Partially freeze the silverside for 1 hour: this will make it much easier to slice it into strips. After this time, remove the meat from the freezer and slice it into 2cm thick strips following the grain of the muscle fibres. You're looking to cut long strips the full length of the muscle because these will eventually dry out and shrink by about a quarter.

2 Salt the silverside strips generously and chill for at least 4 hours in a non-reactive tray, covered with cling film. Laying the strips on top of each other draws out surface moisture, and kicks off the curing process.

3 When the silverside strips have nearly finished chilling, add the vinegar, Worcestershire sauce, bourbon, garlic powder, half the peppercorns, half the coriander seeds and half the chilli flakes to a bowl. Mix well and set aside.

4 Brush off as much salt from the silverside strips as possible. Rinse and dry the tray and place the meat strips back into it. Pour the wet mixture evenly over the strips and return them to the fridge to soak overnight.

5 The next day, mix the remaining peppercorns, coriander seeds and chilli flakes in a bowl. Drain the wet mixture off the silverside strips. Pat the strips dry with kitchen paper and sprinkle the remaining spices on the strips, pushing them into the meat firmly to form a crust on all sides.

6 The meat is now ready to be hung in your drying cabinet or dehydrator. It will take the meat a few days and up to 2 weeks to dry out, depending on the conditions in the box. Once the strips have turned black and start to snap under pressure, they're ready to be set upon. Store the jerky in a cool, dry place and consume it within 1 week. If you plan to make a large batch, then you can freeze any spare jerky for up to 3 months.

TURKEY JERKY

The mild flavour of turkey makes a perfect starting point, then you add your favourite flavours. It is also lower in fat than beef jerky. If you do not own a dehydrator, you can use your oven on the lowest setting and leave the oven door slightly ajar for air circulation.

MAKES 1.5KG

2kg large turkey breast, skin and fat removed

2 tbsp soy sauce

1 tsp Louisiana Hot Sauce (see page 175), or Tabasco sauce

125ml Worcestershire sauce

2 tsp smoked hot or sweet paprika

2 tsp dried sage

2 tsp soft light brown sugar

2 tbsp Basic Dry Rub (see page 16)

1 Partially freeze the turkey breast for 1 hour: this will make it much easier to work with. After 1 hour, slice the meat following the grain of the muscle fibres into strips about 1cm thick, along the full length of the breast.

2 Combine the remaining ingredients in a large Ziplock bag.

3 Add the turkey strips to the bag, making sure all the strips are covered in the marinade. Remove as much air from the bag as possible before sealing, then leave it in the fridge overnight.

4 The next day, remove the turkey strips from the marinade and pat them dry with kitchen paper. Less is more in this case, so aim to remove most of the spice from the strips otherwise they will overpower the turkey flavour.

5 If using a drying cabinet or dehydrator, hang the strips and dehydrate until the turkey jerky is leathery and chewy but not crisp enough to snap when bent. Thinner strips should take 4-7 days to dry; thicker strips up to 10 days. If using an oven, hang the strips from wooden skewers suspended from the top rack. Make sure there is a lot of space between each strip and that they are not touching one another. Using an oven is a much faster method for dehydrating jerky, but can dry out the jerky if dried too fast. We're not 'cooking' the turkey, so you want the warm air to circulate over the strips only to dehydrate them. To do this, leave the oven door ajar to allow the hot air to escape. (You can use a ball of aluminium foil to prop the door open if necessary.) It shouldn't take more than 6-10 hours at an internal oven temperature of about 100°C/Gas ¼. (You can use an oven thermometer to check the internal temperature.)

6 Store the jerky in sealed bags in the fridge if planning to eat within 1 week, or in the freezer for up to 3 months.

THE PERFECT BURGER PATTY AND THE ART OF CLOSHING

More fat means more flavour, and getting the right ratio of meat to fat in a burger patty is easy - if you know how. You need a patty that has at least 20 per cent fat. We use chuck steak (braising steak) and mince it on a medium-coarse blade so it has structure on bite-through. Closhing will help melt all the flavours of your burger together and is easy to do at home on the grill. All you need is a large frying pan and a metal dome, such as an upturned metal mixing bowl, to help create a steamy environment.

MAKES 4 BURGERS

600g chuck steak with about 20 per cent fat content, minced on medium-coarse blade

300g smoked streaky bacon, minced on fine blade

25ml Worcestershire sauce

1 tbsp salted butter, plus extra for buttering the buns

1 large white onion, sliced into rounds

4 tsp Kansas City BBQ Sauce (see page 174), or your favourite ready-made sauce

8 slices burger cheese

8 slices streaky bacon, peppered

4 large glazed unsweetened brioche or potato buns, sliced in half and very lightly buttered

4 tsp mayonnaise

2 Pickled Cucumbers (see page 181), sliced into rounds

4 tsp yellow American mustard

flaked sea salt and freshly ground black pepper

1 Place the steak, bacon and Worcestershire sauce in a bowl and mix well with your hands. Form into 4 patties and place them on a tray lined with a sheet of greaseproof paper. Place the patties in the fridge for 30 minutes to firm up.

2 Melt the butter in a frying pan over a low heat. Add the onion slices, except 4, and fry until golden brown. Set aside on kitchen paper to drain the fat off. Pull the burger patties out of the fridge and leave them to rest until they reach room temperature. Prepare your grill for direct heat on high.

3 Before you grill the burger patties, push your thumb into the middle of each one to create a deep dimple (but be careful not to create a hole). This will help the patties to cook evenly. Season liberally with salt and pepper and place the on the grill.

4 Grill each patty for 2-3 minutes on each side, or until they are cooked to medium. After you have flipped the patties, place a teaspoon of BBQ sauce on the cooked side and top each patty with 2 cheese slices. Place the peppered bacon slices on the grill, and cook until crispy.

5 Meanwhile, place your griddle or frying pan directly over the heat of the grill and let it heat through fully. Toast each of the burger bun halves on the grill for 1 minute or so. Spread the bottom buns with 1 teaspoon of mayonnaise, top with a thin slice of raw onion and a few slices of pickled cucumbers. Place the bottoms on serving plates.

CONTINUED

Bun choice is personal, but avoid anything with an overly chewy crumb or tough crust. We like unsweetened brioche or potato buns. Pretzel rolls (see page 144) are great too, but you will need to steam them using the closhing method, right.

6 Spread 1 teaspoon of mustard on the top halves of the buns and set the top halves aside. Turn over the bacon and crisp the other side. Once ready, place 2 rashers on each patty, over the cheese. Now it's time to build the burgers and closh!

7 Place 1 tablespoon of fried onions on each patty over the bacon, then place the top half of the bun on top of each patty. With a spatula, pick up the patty from the grill and place in the middle of the hot frying pan, ensuring you leave enough space on the outside of the pan to place the metal mixing bowl in the pan without touching the burger patties. Add a few tablespoons of water to the frying pan, and cover with the mixing bowl, creating a steamy environment to help melt the cheese and add moisture to the bun top. After about 15 seconds, remove the mixing bowl (without burning yourself!) and place the bun tops on the bottom buns on the serving plates. Allow the burgers to rest for a few minutes, then serve.

THE #REDSDONUTBURGER

We discovered a version of this burger on our 2012 US BBQ Pilgrimage at a smokehouse joint in Memphis, Tennessee. Otherwise known as the 'Luther Burger', legend has it that this was one of singer-songwriter Luther Vandross's favourite riders for his shows.

A cardiologist's worst nightmare, this burger has been the third-biggest selling item on our menu since February 2013, and contains up to 2,000 calories when fully loaded. This is the holy union of sweet and meat, people, and you're either going to love it or hate it.

MAKES 4 DONUTBURGERS

Dirty Mayo

2 tbsp mayonnaise

1 tbsp prepared English mustard

1 tsp red wine vinegar

1 tsp Worcestershire sauce

¼ tsp dried oregano

¼ tsp salt

¼ tsp ground coriander

¼ tsp garlic powder

¼ tsp onion powder

½ tsp cracked black peppercorns

½ tsp sweet paprika

Fried onions

1 medium white onion, halved and thinly sliced

1 tsp fine sea salt

1 tbsp plain flour

500ml vegetable oil, for shallow frying

Patties

900g chuck steak with about 20 per cent fat content, minced on medium-coarse blade

25ml Worcestershire sauce

4 tsp Kansas City BBQ Sauce (see page 174), or your favourite ready-made sauce

8 slices burger cheese

8 slices streaky bacon, peppered

olive oil, for brushing

8 glazed donuts

flaked sea salt and freshly ground black pepper

1 Make the Dirty Mayo by combining all the ingredients in a bowl and mix well. This is not our epic 'Dirty Sauce' recipe, but a much simpler one that you can rustle up at home.

2 Squeeze any excess moisture from the thinly sliced onions using kitchen paper. Place them in a bowl, sprinkle with the salt, and toss to coat. Add the flour to the bowl and toss the onions again. Heat the vegetable oil in a frying pan over a medium heat. Add the onions and fry them until crisp. Remove them from the frying pan with a slotted spoon and set them aside on kitchen paper.

3 Place the chuck mince and Worcestershire sauce in a bowl and mix well with your hands. Form into 8 even-sized patties, place on a baking sheet lined with greaseproof paper and transfer to the fridge for 30 minutes to firm up. After this time, pull the burger patties out of the fridge and leave them to rest until they reach room temperature. Prepare your grill for direct heat on high.

4 Before you grill the burger patties, push your thumb into the middle of each patty to create a dimple but be careful not to create a hole. This will help the patties cook evenly. Place the patties on the grill and season them liberally with salt and pepper. Cook for 1-2 minutes on one side. After you have flipped the patties, place half a teaspoon of BBQ sauce on the cooked side and top each patty with 1 slice of cheese. Cook for a further 1-2 minutes or until just medium.

5 Whilst the patties are being grilled, place the peppered bacon slices on the grill, and cook until crispy. Brush oil on each side of the donuts and place on the grill to toast on both sides. Set aside, covered, to keep warm. Turn over the bacon and crisp the other side. Once ready, place 2 rashers on each of the patties, on top of the cheese layer. You're now ready to build the awesome #DONUTBURGER.

6 Place a donut on a serving plate and top with a layer of patty, BBQ sauce and cheese from the grill. Now place a second layer of patty, BBQ sauce and cheese (this time with bacon) on top of the first layer and crown it all with the second donut. Fill the donut hole with the Dirty Mayo and anoint the sauce with the crispy onions to add a decadent, crunchy texture. If you wish, adorn the #REDSDONUTBURGER with a custom-made flag. We did.

TEAM RED'S SMOKED OX CHEEK AND CANOE-CUT MARROWBONES
(DOUBLE 'COOK'S CHOICE' AWARD WINNER)

This recipe won Red's a couple of firsts on the UK's BBQ competition circuit and offered up the idea that BBQ could be fine dining if you put your mind to it. There are several components to this dish, including a brioche box loaf, which needs to be prepared the night before, a low and slow-smoked ox cheek, red onion marmalade, red wine jus and canoe-cut veal bones.

STAGE 1

SERVES 6

Brioche box loaf

2 x 7g sachets fast action dried yeast

1 tbsp tepid water

300g plain flour, plus extra for dusting

4 room-temperature eggs, lightly beaten

170g unsalted butter, softened, plus extra for greasing

50g caster sugar

2 tsp salt

1 Dissolve the sachets of yeast in the tepid water in a small bowl and set aside for 10-20 minutes until the yeast begins to froth.

2 Sift the flour into the bowl of a stand mixer. Add the eggs, butter, sugar, salt and dissolved yeast. Using the dough hook attachment at a medium speed, mix until a smooth dough has formed and is coming away from the sides of the bowl. This may take 5 minutes or so.

3 Take the dough out of the bowl, roll it into a ball and place it inside a container twice its size. Cover loosely with cling film and transfer to the fridge overnight to rise.

4 The next day, grease a 450g loaf tin. Roll out the still chilled dough on a floured flat surface. Fold the dough over itself four times and then roll it out again. Repeat this process 4 times.

5 Cut the dough into 4 even-sized pieces. Take each piece and roll it into a ball, then divide this into two. Continue this process until there are 8 dough balls of an equal size.

6 Set the balls into the greased loaf tin. Place the tin in a warm place and leave at room temperature for 30 minutes to 1 hour until the dough has risen to the top. Don't try to rush the proving by putting the dough in too warm a place; this will only melt the butter and prevent a good rise during the bake. Just before you are ready to bake the bread, preheat the oven to 150°C/Gas 2. Place the tin on the middle shelf of the oven and bake for 20-25 minutes, or until the loaf has a golden brown crust.

7 Remove the tin from the oven and leave it to cool for 5 minutes before removing the loaf and setting it on a wire rack. Cover it with a clean kitchen paper and leave it to cool completely while you work on the other stages of the dish.

CONTINUED

STAGE II

Low and slow smoked
ox cheek

1kg ox cheeks, trimmed of excess fat

20g yellow American mustard

20g caster sugar

50g Beef Coffee Rub (see page 17)

100ml Worcestershire sauce

100ml water

WOOD

About 4 decent-sized chunks of air-
dried oak all soaked in water overnight
or for at least 2 hours.

1 Set your smoker for indirect smoking at 110°C (225°F). Place the trimmed ox cheeks in a bowl. Rub the mustard and then the sugar on to the meat, working it in well so you get an even covering over the meat. Place it in the smoker, and then add 2 chunks of wood to the coals. Smoke for up to 3 hours. In the meantime, mix the Worcestershire sauce and water in a clean, sterilised spray bottle to make a spritz.

2 When the internal temperature of the meat reaches 60°C (140°F), remove it from the smoker and wrap it in aluminium foil, along with about 2 tablespoons of the spritz to retain moisture and accelerate the cooking time. Return the package to the smoker for another 2 hours, or until the meat reaches an internal temperature of 92°C (197°F). (It needs to reach this high temperature so the meat can be pulled.) While the ox cheeks are smoking, continue with the next stages.

STAGE III

Red onion marmalade

1kg red onions, peeled and thinly sliced

500g soft light brown sugar

grated zest and juice of ½ orange
(about 50ml)

200ml red wine vinegar

1 Place the onions in a heavy-based saucepan over a medium heat. Add the sugar, orange zest and juice and red wine vinegar and give it a stir. Bring it to the boil, and then reduce the heat to a simmer for about 15 minutes, or until the onions have stewed and the liquid has evaporated leaving a shiny, moist, but not runny, onion jam. Remove from the heat and set aside to cool.

STAGE IV

Red wine jus

1 tsp olive oil

25g unsalted butter

1 celery stick, finely diced

1 medium carrot, finely diced

1 medium onion, finely diced

4 cloves garlic, crushed

2 large glasses red wine

1 tomato, quartered

2 sprigs fresh thyme

2 beef stock cubes

1 litre boiling water

1 tsp tomato purée

1 tbsp redcurrant jelly

salt and freshly ground black pepper

1 Heat the oil and butter in a saucepan over a medium heat. Add the vegetables and garlic and fry until they begin to caramelise: they should be brown. Stir in 1 glass of wine, then leave to reduce a little, but do not let the pan go dry.

2 Add the tomato and thyme sprigs, and continue cooking until the tomato starts to break down and go a little mushy.

3 Meanwhile, dissolve the beef stock cubes in the boiled water and add to the saucepan, along with the tomato purée. Bring the whole lot to the boil, reduce the heat and simmer until the volume of the stock has reduced by half. Strain the stock through a fine sieve. Do not force anything through, but let it drain naturally.

4 Pour the remaining glass of red wine into a clean saucepan over a medium heat, and simmer until it reduces by half. Whisk in the redcurrant jelly to blend, and stir in the strained stock. Leave the mixture to simmer until it reduces by half again and you have a thick glossy sauce.

STAGE V

Grilled canoe-cut marrow bone

6 canoe-cut beef shin bones, 15–20cm long

BBQ sauce (use your favourite)

sea salt and freshly ground black pepper

1 Set your barbecue for direct grilling, and chuck in a wood chunk and close the lid of the smoker. Season the bones with salt and pepper. Place them on the grill rack, bone-side down, but arrange them on the perimeter of the coal bed.

2 Grill for 10 minutes, or until the marrow has set into a jelly.

BUILDING THE AWARD-WINNING DISH

1 Pull the smoked ox cheeks into long strands, but not too much or it will become like a stew. Add just enough red wine jus to loosen up the gelatinous meat. Keep this warm on top of or inside the smoker while you work on the other elements of the dish.

2 Cut the brioche loaf into 12 slices, and set them on the grill. Toast on both sides, being careful not to burn the bread.

3 Take the canoes, which should be ready by now, off the grill and spoon over the pulled ox cheek, dividing the meat evenly between all the bones. Top each bone with a heaped tablespoon of the red onion marmalade and finish by serving each bone with 2 slices of toasted brioche, cut into triangles.

GRILLING DIRTY WITH A TOMAHAWK

On special occasions, like Father's Day, we'll roll out the Tomahawks. You can see where the 'Tomahawk' element comes into this recipe, but probably not the 'Dirty', which is when chunks of meat are cooked directly on hot coals. With the simple touch of fanning the ashes away from the grey coals before placing the meat on top, the finished product won't be a carbonised lump of toughness. Grilling 'dirty' will give a rustic finish to the pit-dipped meat, but it won't taste dirty! Please note that you must only use lumpwood charcoal when grilling directly. It's best to use thicker cuts of meat, such as lamb rump steaks or extra-thick pork chops.

SERVES 1

1.2kg Tomahawk steak or 700g bone-in rib-eye

2 tbsp unsalted butter

1 tbsp Dijon mustard

2 sprigs fresh rosemary

2 sprigs fresh thyme

1 tsp Smoked Garlic and Herb Crust (see page 23)

flaked sea salt and freshly cracked black peppercorns

1 Prepare a super-hot, level bed of coals with an even layer of grey ash across the top.

2 Season the steak liberally with salt and pepper, working it in as deeply as possible with your hands. Leave to rest for 5 minutes to allow the salt to penetrate the meat. Melt the butter and the mustard in a saucepan near the coals. Once melted, set aside away from the fire.

3 Using a hand-held fan or hair dryer, blow all of the grey ash away from the bed of coals, making sure you have a clear path in the direction you are blowing the hot ash. Once the coals are completely clear of ash, baste the meat on all sides with the melted mustard butter and press half of the rosemary and thyme sprigs into one side of the meat. Place the meat, herb-side down, directly on the coals and cook for 1 minute. Rotate the meat by 90 degrees to cook the next side and repeat until all four sides have been grilled for 1 minute each.

4 Remove the steak from the coals, brushing off any coals that might be sticking to the meat, and place the steak on a serving board. Discard any burnt herbs. Brush more of the butter mixture all over the meat and push the remaining herbs into one side of the meat.

5 Fan the coals again to remove any unwanted ash build-up. Set the meat back on the hot coal bed and cook for 1 minute per side as before, or until the internal temperature of the steak reads 45°C (113°F) on a digital probe thermometer.

6 Remove the steak from the coals and brush off any coals sticking to the meat. Leave to rest for 5 minutes, slice on the angle and lightly sprinkle with the herb crust.

BUTTERFLIED LEG OF LAMB

Leg of lamb is mainly a lean cut of meat, so it's perfect for cooking fast and furious until it develops a crispy exterior while maintaining a juicy, pink medium-rare centre. Butterfly the lamb by removing the bone with a sharp knife and flatten out the meat so it cooks evenly, by slashing lines deep into the thicker end.

SERVES 8

1 leg of lamb, approximately 6kg

3 tbsp Cabrito Dry Rub (see page 18)

12-16 baby new potatoes

olive oil, for drizzling

2 tbsp Smoked Garlic and Herb Crust (see page 23)

fine sea salt and freshly ground black pepper

Yoghurt dipper

300g natural yoghurt

2 tbsp fresh lime juice

2 cloves garlic, peeled

3 tbsp roughly chopped fresh mint leaves, plus extra for garnishing

1 tsp cayenne pepper

WOOD

3–4 wood chunks, such as cherry or oak, soaked in water overnight or for at least 2 hours

1 First, strain the yoghurt. Line a medium-large bowl with a piece of muslin, or a clean dishcloth. Dump the yoghurt into the centre of the cloth, bring the four corners together and lift it up. Twist the corners to squeeze the liquid into the bowl. Continue squeezing, putting the yoghurt under pressure to force the liquid out. Place the squeezed cloth with the yoghurt in a sieve or colander. Set the sieve or colander in a bowl where it doesn't touch the bottom, so that the liquid can continue to drain. Leave to drain in the fridge for 2-3 hours.

2 Place the leg of lamb, meatier-side down, on a large chopping board. Use your fingers to locate the bone. With a flexible, sharp knife, slice along the length of the leg to the bone and then around it. Scrape the meat away from the bone as closely as possible. Continue to work your knife around the bone, lifting it free with your other hand. Once de-boned, part the entire leg down the middle with the knife, being careful not to slice all the way through to the board. Trim away any unwanted fat or sinew and then make deep slashes into the thicker end, butterflying it out to make the whole hunk of meat the same thickness from end to end.

3 Work the dry rub into the meat, massaging it into the crevices with your fingers, then leave it to marinate at room temperature for 20-30 minutes. Prepare your grill for direct high heat at 150-170°C (300-350°F) and cover with the lid. Place the potatoes in a bowl, drizzle them with oil and toss to coat. Season with salt and pepper to taste and set aside.

4 When the lamb is ready, add the soaked wood chunks to the coals, place the lamb on the grill and close the lid. Place the potatoes on the grill around the lamb. Keep an eye on the internal temperature of the grill.

5 After 30 minutes of hot smoking, remove the lid and flip the meat over. If the potatoes are fully cooked, push them to the edge of the grill to keep warm. If they need more time, place them closer to the coals and then move them to the side once fully cooked.

CONTINUED

6 Grill the meat, without the lid on, for a further 30 minutes, moving the leg around the grill frequently for a crispy finish. If you like your lamb cooked medium, when the internal temperature of the lamb approaches 60°C (140°F), remove it from the grill and set it aside to rest (the internal temperature will continue to rise due to the 'afterburn' effect (see page 12). If you prefer your lamb medium-well done, then wait until it reaches an internal temperature of 65°C (150°F), once rested. If you don't have a digital probe thermometer, simply cut into the meat and look inside. Within seconds you'll know how it's doing.

7 Once the meat has reached your desired internal temperature, take the meat off the grill, cover it loosely with aluminium foil, and let it rest for a while to allow the internal juices to redistribute. Resting times vary, but assume 1 minute for each 100g of cooked weight. Remove the potatoes from the grill and keep them warm.

8 While the lamb is resting, place the strained yoghurt, lime juice and garlic in a blender and purée on high speed until blended. While blending, slowly incorporate the mint and season with salt, pepper and cayenne. Remove from the blender and scrape the mixture into a bowl.

9 Place the rested lamb on a wooden serving board and slice it on an angle to expose the juicy, pink centre then arrange the slices on a serving platter. Sprinkle the garlic and herb crust onto the lamb slices. Cut the potatoes in half, mix them into the meat juices on the board and add them to the platter.

10 Dollop the yoghurt dipper into the gaps between the meat and the potatoes on the platter and top with freshly chopped mint. Tuck in (with your hands, preferably).

LOW AND SLOW SMOKED MUTTON SHOULDER AND LEXINGTON DIPPER

Kentucky is famous for bourbon, horse racing, bluegrass music and some Colonel fella who did something with fried chicken (it'll probably never catch on). But Kentuckians also have a unique approach to BBQ. They use mutton, and it is usually served with a BBQ sauce spiked with Worcestershire sauce to cut through the strongly flavoured meat. Get out your five-string banjo, sup some bourbon and start cooking.

SERVES 10-12

125g freshly ground black pepper

2½ tbsp soft dark brown sugar

2 tbsp flaked sea salt

½ tsp ground allspice

2 cloves garlic, crushed

4kg mutton shoulder, bone in and trimmed of excess fat

60ml Worcestershire sauce

60ml cider vinegar

60ml water

Lexington Dipper

80ml Worcestershire sauce

125g ketchup

80ml cider vinegar

3 tbsp soft dark brown sugar

1 tsp mild hot sauce

1 tsp freshly ground black pepper

2 tsp fresh lemon juice

½ tsp fine sea salt

½ tsp onion salt

½ tsp garlic powder

¼ tsp ground allspice

WOOD

4 oak wood chunks, soaked in water overnight or for at least 2 hours

1 Place all the dipper ingredients in a large saucepan over a high heat whilst mixing with a wooden spoon. Bring the mixture to the boil. Once it has reached boiling point, remove it from the heat and leave it to cool.

2 When you are ready to cook, set your smoker for indirect smoking at 110°C (225°F).

3 Place the salt, sugar, salt, allspice and garlic in a mixing bowl and stir them together to make a rub. Apply this generously to the mutton, making sure to rub it well into all the meat. Put the mutton shoulder into the smoker, fat-side down. Chuck a few chunks of wood on the coals to up the smoke levels, and close the lid of the smoker. Add the Worcestershire sauce, cider vinegar and water to a clean, sterilised spray bottle to make a spritz.

4 Typically you need to cook the mutton for 3 hours for each kilo of meat. Because this is shoulder, you're in it for the long haul. It's very important to spray the mutton every hour with the spritz to help break down the fats that are rendering out of the meat, leaving behind a sweet, firm bark.

5 When the meat reaches an internal temperature of 76°C (168°F), remove it from the smoker, wrap it in a double layer of aluminium foil and set aside in a warm place to rest. The meat is lovely served sliced in a bun with a side of the dipper.

MAKE YOUR OWN...
LINKS

TEXAS HOTLINKS

To make fresh sausage, all you need is meat, seasonings, skins and a mincer. Sausage skins can be ordered from your butcher, and usually come in a range of gauges. We use large pork skins for our hotlinks and smaller sheep skins for our jerky sausage. Always partially freeze your meat and fat for 1 hour or so before mincing, to prevent the fat from melting during the mincing process.

MAKES 16-20 LARGE SAUSAGES

2.5m medium-gauge hog sausage skins

1.5kg pork shoulder

500g pork back fat

500g braising steak

60g fine sea salt

80g soft light brown sugar

2 tbsp fennel seeds, toasted

4 tbsp fresh cracked black pepper

½ tsp freshly grated nutmeg

200g fresh parsley, finely chopped

100g garlic, peeled and chopped

200ml beer (lager)

60ml sherry vinegar

1 tbsp cayenne pepper

1 tbsp dried chilli flakes

1 tbsp yellow mustard seeds

1 tbsp cracked black peppercorns

1 Soak the skins in water to remove the salt while you prepare the sausage meat. Cut the pork shoulder, back fat and steak into 2.5cm cubes and freeze for 1 hour.

2 Place the salt, sugar, fennel seeds, pepper, nutmeg, parsley and garlic in a large bowl and mix well to combine. Stir in the beer and sherry vinegar and set aside.

3 Mince the meat on the coarse setting and add to a bowl. Mix with the cayenne pepper, chilli flakes, mustard seeds and black pepper.

4 Test the seasoning by frying up a small batch, taste and adjust the seasoning of the meat mixture accordingly.

5 Cut off a piece of sausage skin about 1 metre long. Attach the sausage-stuffer to the mincer, and roll on the wet skin, leaving a good amount of skin hanging off the end that you can twist into sausages. Don't pack the skins too tightly, and avoid air gaps where possible.

6 Once the skin has been stuffed, twist it into links about 25cm long, changing twisting directions every other link. Using kitchen scissors, snip the links (it is much easier to smoke and turn individual sausages). Repeat the process with the remaining stuffing-meat and skin. Place the finished sausages in a covered dish and refrigerate.

7 Prepare your barbecue for indirect heat around 60°C (140°F). Bring the sausages to room temperature then oil them and place in the smoker for around 3 hours. You want to start the cooking at a lower temperature for about 30 minutes, then increase the smoking temperature to 100°C (212°F) for the rest of the cooking.

JALAPEÑO CHEDDAR LINKS

We first had these at Black's BBQ in Lockhart, Texas, on one of our early road trips and they blew our tiny minds. Since 1932, Black's sausages have been hand-tied, hanged and smoked to perfection over oak in their impressive smokers out back. The addition of melting cheese chunks and spicy jalapeños in this sausage recipe will, hopefully, also blow your mind!

MAKES 10-12 LARGE SAUSAGES

2 metres medium-gauge hog sausage skins

1.5kg beef brisket

300g pork back fat

50g flaked sea salt, crushed

1 tbsp cracked black peppercorns

125ml white wine vinegar

500g mild Cheddar cheese, cut into ½cm cubes

80g cloves garlic, chopped

4 medium-size fresh jalapeños or green chillies, finely chopped (remove the seeds if you prefer it less spicy)

1 tbsp dried chilli flakes (reduce to 1 tsp if you prefer it less spicy)

200ml lager or beer

100ml sherry vinegar

1 Soak the skins in water to remove the salt while you prepare the sausage meat. Cut the beef and pork back fat into 1cm cubes and freeze for 1 hour. This will make the mincing process much easier.

2 Combine the salt, pepper, vinegar, cheese, garlic, jalapeños and chilli flakes in a large bowl and mix well. Stir in the lager or beer and sherry vinegar.

3 Mince the beef and fat on the coarse setting. Add to the bowl with the cheese mixture and stir thoroughly.

4 Take a small patty of the mixture and place it in a frying pan over a medium heat. When it has cooked, taste it for seasoning. It may need a little more salt or black pepper, so season to taste.

5 Cut off a piece of hog skin about 1 metre long. Attach the sausage-stuffer to the mincer, and roll on the wet skin, leaving a good amount of skin hanging off the end that you can twist into sausages once filled. Don't pack the skins too tightly, and avoid air gaps where possible.

6 Twist into links about 20cm long, changing twisting directions every other link. Using kitchen scissors, snip the links (it is much easier to smoke and turn individual sausages). Repeat the process with the remaining stuffing-meat and skin. Place the finished sausages in a dish and cover with cling film. Refrigerate the sausages for a few hours.

7 Prepare your barbecue for indirect heat at around 60°C (140°F). Take the sausages out of the fridge and bring to room temperature for about 30 minutes. Then oil the sausages and place them in the smoker for around 3 hours. You want to start the cooking at a lower temperature for about 30 minutes, then increase the smoking temperature to 100°C (212°F) for the rest of the cooking.

8 Test the sausages occasionally with a digital probe thermometer. After around 3 hours, or when the internal temperature of the sausages reaches 72°C (161°F), they are ready. These links are great on their own, and even better while supping a cold beer!

OAK-SMOKED STICKY CHICKEN

The key to achieving moist chicken is to ensure the white meat and dark meat on the bird are ready at the same time after cooking. If you're using jointed pieces, remember that the dark meat (thighs and legs) take longer than the white meat (breast), so start grilling the dark meat first.

SERVES 4

2 x 1.5kg free-range chickens

4 tbsp Bay Poultry Rub (see page 18)

200g Kansas City BBQ Sauce
(see page 174), plus extra for serving

4 Pickled Cucumbers (see page 181),
quartered

Brine

2 litres warm water

300g sea salt

300g soft dark brown sugar

4 cloves garlic, crushed

4 whole cloves

2 dried bay leaves

WOOD

4 oak wood chunks, soaked in water
overnight or for at least 2 hours

1 First, make your brine. Use a deep bowl or container large enough to hold the brine while submerging the two halved chickens. Add all of the brine ingredients to the bowl and stir until the sugar and salt have dissolved. Set aside while you halve the chickens.

2 Using heavy-duty kitchen scissors, starting from the rear end of the bird, cut very close along one side of the backbone, all the way up to neck. Repeat on the other side to remove the spine. Flip the bird over, open it up and flatten it out. Cut through the middle of the breasts, pushing through the wishbone, slicing the chicken in half. Fully submerge the halves in the brine. Cover loosely with cling film and leave in the fridge for 12 hours.

3 When you are ready to cook, prepare your grill for indirect heat at 110-140°C (225-275°F).

4 Lift the chicken halves out of the brine and dry them off with kitchen paper. Make a few slashes into the legs and the thighs all the way to the bone to cook evenly (don't slash the breasts). Massage the poultry rub deep into the chicken so it's well covered on both sides, pushing the rub into the slashes. Leave aside to marinate for 10 minutes.

5 Add the soaked wood chunks to the coals and position your chicken halves on the opposite side to the coals, for indirect smoking. Close the grill lid and leave to smoke for 2-3 hours. If needed, add more logs or chips to keep the smoke churning.

6 After 2 hours, use a digital probe thermometer to check the internal temperature: once it reaches 72°C (161°F), flip the chooks over so they are skin-side down, but this time place them directly over the coals for a few seconds to crisp the skin. Once crispy, flip them back over and place them on the indirect side of the grill. Glaze the smoked chickens generously with BBQ sauce and smoke for a further 20 minutes with the lid on.

7 Check the internal temperature, and when the meat reaches 75°C (167°F), take it off of the grill and let it rest for 5 minutes. Joint the rested chicken and top with more BBQ sauce and serve alongside some slaw and pickles. Tuck in!.

DIRTY-PLANKED SPATCHCOCK CHICKEN

You don't get much quicker than cooking meat directly on a bed of hot coals! Dirty, bourbon-brined chicken finished on a steaming plank of cedar wood, loaded with fresh herbs, lemon and a bourbon-pickle salt crust. By butterflying the bird, you'll be able to cook a whole chicken in less than 40 minutes. And remember: only use lumpwood charcoal when grilling dirty.

SERVES 2-3

2kg free-range chicken

2 tbsp Old Bay-style Rub (see page 20)

3 sprigs fresh tarragon, leaves picked

6 leaves fresh sage

3 sprigs fresh rosemary, leaves picked

juice of ½ lemon

2 tsp Pickleback Crust (see page 23)

Brine

2 litres warm water

200ml bourbon (or whisky)

300g sea salt

300g soft dark brown sugar

4 cloves garlic, crushed

2 dried bay leaves

Baste

100ml extra virgin olive oil

50ml fresh lemon juice

75g unsalted butter

1 tbsp caster sugar

2 garlic cloves, crushed

1 tsp onion granules

WOOD

Plank of untreated cedar wood, that will fit inside the smoker, soaked in water overnight (or for at least 3–4 hours) and oiled

1 The day before you are ready to cook, make the brine. Use a deep bowl large enough to hold the brine while submerging the chicken. Add all of the ingredients and stir until the sugar and salt have dissolved. Set aside.

2 Place the chicken on a chopping board and remove the backbone (see page 94). Flip the bird over, open it up and push down to flatten it out. Place in the brine and weigh it down with a plate to submerge it fully. Leave to marinate in the fridge for 12 hours.

3 The following day, prepare your barbecue with a flat bed of super-hot coals. Make the chicken baste by combining all the ingredients in a saucepan and heat directly on the coals, stirring constantly. Remove the saucepan from the heat and set aside.

4 Remove the chicken from the brine, discard the liquid and dry with kitchen paper. Make a few slashes in the legs and thighs all the way to the bone. Massage the rub all over the chicken and into the slashes. Skewer the chicken from the thigh to the opposite wing, on both sides. This will prevent the chicken from bowing. Leave to marinate for 10 minutes.

5 Fan the grey ash from the hot coal bed and, using a brush, paint the chicken on all sides with the baste mixture. Place the chicken directly on the coals for 2 minutes, baste the top, flip over and baste the surface again, and cook for a further 2 minutes. Repeat this process twice more, so the total cooking time is 12 minutes.

6 Transfer the chicken to the prepared cedar plank, brushing off any small coal pieces on the chicken. Allow it to rest for 5 minutes then baste again. Place the plank directly on the coal bed. Cover the grill with a lid to create a smoky atmosphere. Cook for a further 10 minutes, or until the chicken juices run clear between the leg and the thigh.

7 Once cooked, remove the chicken and plank from the barbecue and leave it to rest for 10 minutes on the plank, catching and reserving any juices. Transfer the spatchcock to a serving board. Mix the fresh herbs and lemon juice with the resting juices and chop finely. Scatter the herbs and the Pickleback Crust over the chicken.

BBQ CHICKEN WINGS

In the restaurant, our chicken wings are showers not growers. They have to be as big as you can get them, and never jointed. At Red's we straighten ours, and serve them with blue cheese dip and sticks of celery. The combination of the strong blue cheese, smoky wings, sweet BBQ sauce and crunch of the celery is heavenly. The wings don't take long to smoke, and can keep in the fridge for a few days, perfect for that leftovers lunch in the office.

SERVES 4

12 jumbo or 20 regular chicken wings

50g Old Bay-style Rub
(see page 20)

100g Kansas City BBQ Sauce
(see page 174)

200g soured cream

150g mayonnaise

pinch of salt and ground white pepper

100g blue cheese

4 celery sticks

1 To straighten each wing, break the bones at the bends and, to keep them straight during the smoke, snip or slice the connecting skin, which will shrink as it cooks. Place the wings in a large bowl and sprinkle over the poultry rub. Toss the wings to coat. Leave them to marinate while you prepare your smoker to cook at 120°C (250°F).

2 Add the wings to the smoker, leaving enough space between them so that they get a good lick of smoke. The wings will take 1½-2 hours to cook. It is extremely important that the internal temperature of the thickest part of the wing (near the bone) reaches at least 72°C (161°F).

3 After 1 hour or so, brush some BBQ sauce on to all the wings, and continue to smoke for another 15 minutes, then flip all the wings over and repeat. If any of the wings have started to fold back into shape, straighten them out before putting on the sticky BBQ sauce.

4 During the cooking, make the blue cheese dip. If you have a hand-held stick blender or food processor, this recipe couldn't be simpler. Put the soured cream, mayo, salt and pepper into the bowl or jug of the processor, and then crumble in the blue cheese. Blend until you have a smooth, creamy sauce.

5 Serve the wings with blue cheese dip and crunchy celery.

BUTTERFLIED SMOKED TURKEY

We're all creatures of habit, but at Christmas time things can get a little repetitive. If you're looking to stay true to tradition, but want to change it up a little and surprise the family, give this Smoked Turkey recipe a crack. It's an annual special at Red's during the festive period and always goes down a treat. Everyone knows how dry turkey breast meat can be, and because we are cooking thighs and breast together, the risk of dry meat is high. To help this, an injection of honey, melted butter and garlic powder is administered before the smoke. You can buy meat injectors online easily enough.

SERVES 10-12

6kg fresh (not frozen) turkey

4 litres brine (see page 94)

200g Old Bay-style Poultry Rub
(see page 20)

150g unsalted butter, melted

Injection

100ml clear honey

10g garlic powder

100g unsalted melted butter

6g ground white pepper

WOOD

4 oak wood chunks soaked overnight
or for at least 2 hours

1 Separate the skin of the turkey from the meat. This will help the brine to penetrate the meat, allow you to apply a rub directly on the meat, and also help achieve a crispy skin. Start at the neck. Cut off any excess skin and then push your fingertips between the skin and the meat, working your way down the breast and around the ribcage. For the thighs, start at the opening of the cavity and use the same technique.

2 Pour the brine into a large stockpot or soup pot, or even a clean, used-for-food-only bucket. Add the turkey and submerge it in the liquid. Leave it in the fridge overnight.

3 The following day, set your smoker for indirect smoking at 170°C (325°F). Take the turkey out of the brine, and set it on a large chopping board or work surface. Dry it with kitchen paper. You will need a good sharp cook's knife, about 30cm long, and a strong pair of poultry shears. Check that all of the giblets have been removed then place the knife into the cavity of the bird. Find the edge of its spine on one side. With a lot of pressure and the weight of your body, begin to sever the backbone out of the bird. Repeat the process on the other side of the spine. Use the poultry shears to remove any final bits.

4 Flip the bird over and place your palms between the thighs above the tail end. Using the full weight of your body, press down to flatten out the bird. You should hear its bones crack. If you notice any bits of skin that are loose, you can fix these to the flesh after applying the rub to help stop the skin from pulling off during the smoke. Trim off any excess fat or skin.

CONTINUED

5 Lift up the skin and apply most of the poultry rub on the meat underneath. Any leftover rub can be distributed on top of the bird, but this is not essential. Use wooden cocktail sticks to secure any skin that is flopping about and coming loose. Score a few slits into the top of each thigh and upper leg to help all the parts of the bird cook at the same rate.

6 Now mix all the ingredients for the injection and load your injector. Inject in about 6 places in each breast, and then into each score mark on the legs. Use up all of the injection liquid.

7 Place the turkey on a rack inside a roasting tin and place it in the smoker. Add a few chunks of oak to the coals. The turkey will take approximately 4 hours to cook. The final internal temperature must be no less than 72°C (161°F) for the breast and 79°C (175°F) for the leg and thigh. As a guide, this should take about 35 minutes per kilo but, for safety, rely on your digital probe thermometer.

8 After the first hour of cooking, drench a piece of muslin in melted butter and drape this over the bird. This will prevent the smoke from killing the flavour and will also help crisp up the skin. Every hour or so, use a turkey baster to suck up the juices that have dripped into the tin and use them to baste the turkey.

9 The wings and the ends of the drumsticks will cook much faster than the rest of the bird, so check the temperatures of these after about 2½ hours. Once they have reached 72°C (161°F), wrap them in aluminium foil to stop them burning.

10 When the whole bird has reached the correct internal temperature, remove the turkey from the smoker, lift off the muslin, and loosely cover the turkey with aluminium foil. Leave it to rest for 30 minutes before carving and then serve with your favourite Christmas trimmings, or try some of our BBQ Christmas recipes online at www.truebarbecue.com

CHAPTER

FISH

PLANKED FISH

Fish is a little more delicate than meat, so you need to be gentle when barbecuing it. Throwing fish steaks straight on to the grill will result in disaster, as the fish will begin to flake as it cooks. However, placing the fish skin-side down on an soaked cedar-wood plank and hot-smoking it will not only keep the integrity of the fish, it will also add a smoky, earthy favour. You'll need a lid for the barbecue.

We've used salmon in this recipe, but you can use any firm fish, such as cod, whiting, pollock, halibut or monkfish. If you don't have any South Carolina BBQ Sauce to hand, use a mix of mustard (French, Dijon or American are fine) and brown sugar loosened with some olive oil.

SERVES 4-5

1kg side of salmon or fish steaks

1 tbsp South Carolina BBQ Sauce (see page 169), for basting

olive oil, for brushing the plank

1 tbsp chopped fresh dill

1 lemon, sliced

flaked sea salt and freshly ground black pepper

WOOD

soaked plank of untreated cedar wood (that will fit inside smoker)

chunks of sweet alder cherry or oak wood, soaked in water overnight (or for at least 2 hours)

1   Prepare your barbecue for direct heat grilling at 140°C (275°F). Rinse the salmon or fish steaks and pat dry with kitchen paper. Using a basting brush, paint the BBQ sauce on all sides of the fish. Season with salt and pepper and set aside to marinate for 10 minutes.

2   Add some wood chunks to your barbecue, close the lid and allow the smoke to develop. Oil the soaked plank on one side and arrange the lemon slices over it. Place the fish, skin-side down, on top of the lemon. Place the plank on the grill, directly on the coal bed, and close the lid.

3   Hot-smoke for 20-30 minutes, or until the fish starts to flake and become firm. The centre of the fish should still be pinkish red for medium rare. If you have a digital probe thermometer, check the internal temperature. At 55-60°C (130-140°F) the fish should be done but still moist.

4   Once the fish is cooked, remove it and the plank from the grill, top with the chopped dill, more freshly ground pepper and squeeze two of the lemon quarters all over it. Place the remaining lemon quarters on the side and serve.

STUFFED SQUID WITH PULLED PORK

There are loads of things you can do with leftover smoked pork shoulder, but one of our favourites is to turn it into a simple surf and turf and serve it with some good old Southern-style Grits (see page 164). If you don't have leftover pulled pork, you can use ground pork instead (in the same quantities), but it will need grilling an extra 5-10 minutes as you're using raw meat instead of cooked.

SERVES 4

80g breadcrumbs

100ml whole milk

300g Pulled Pork (see page 36)

2 cloves garlic, crushed

1 tsp fennel seeds, toasted and ground

½ tsp dried chilli flakes

½ tsp flaked sea salt, plus extra for seasoning

¼ tsp coarsely ground black peppercorns, plus extra for seasoning

1 tbsp chopped fresh parsley, plus extra to garnish

4 large whole squid including tentacles, cleaned by your fishmonger

olive oil, for drizzling

1 lemon, quartered

1 fresh red chilli, sliced

1 Place the breadcrumbs in a large bowl. Add the milk and leave to soak. After 5 minutes, add the pork, garlic, fennel, chilli flakes, salt, pepper and parsley. Mix it together gently with your hands. Using a small spoon, loosely stuff each squid body three-quarters full with the mixture and secure the open end with a wooden cocktail stick. Set the stuffed squid on a baking tray lined with greaseproof paper, and place it in the fridge.

2 Prepare your grill for direct cooking over a medium heat. When it is ready, take the squid out of the fridge, drizzle them with olive oil, rubbing it over the squid to coat, and season with salt and pepper. Oil the grill rack, set the squid on the rack and place on the barbecue.

3 While the squid are grilling, place the tentacles in a small bowl and drizzle them with oil. Toss to coat, and then season with salt and pepper. Set aside while you finish cooking the squid. Cook the stuffed squid for about 10 minutes, turning frequently, until they begin to crisp up and turn golden. When they are ready, transfer them to a serving platter.

4 Place the prepared tentacles over the hottest part of the grill for 3 minutes until curled up and crunchy. Add them to the platter.

5 Squeeze a lemon quarter over the squid, sprinkle over the chilli slices and garnish with parsley. Set the remaining lemon quarters alongside the stuffed squid and serve.

FIRE ROCKEFELLER

Imagine you're six days into a meaty US BBQ roadtrip across six states in an enclosed RV filled to the brim with six other festering dudes, plus you've three more days of true barbecue sampling ahead of you. What's the one thing you need most to refresh the palate, other than water and vegetables? Well, just by chance we found ourselves halfway between two meaty stalwarts, Alabama and Texas, in the beautiful city of New Orleans, Louisiana. New Orleans isn't known for its BBQ, but it is known for its seafood, more specifically, its oysters. So, we popped down to ACME Oyster House, queued up for 2 hours and made for some of their famous cheese-bubblingly spicy chargrilled oysters, which was a welcome break for the boys in the RV.

SERVES 2-3

60g unsalted butter

2 cloves garlic, finely chopped

2 shallots, finely chopped

60ml white wine

60g grated Parmesan cheese

1 tbsp chopped fresh chervil, plus extra to garnish

1 tbsp chopped fresh parsley, plus extra to garnish

dash of Louisiana Hot Sauce (see page 175), plus extra to serve

2 tbsp olive oil

80g breadcrumbs

12 oysters, on the half shell

lemon wedges, to serve

salt and freshly ground black pepper

1 Prepare your barbecue with an even bed of hot coals. Let the coals grey over with ash.

2 Melt the butter in a frying pan on the side of the coals. Add the garlic and shallots and fry gently for 2 minutes to infuse the flavours. Deglaze the pan with the white wine, then add the Parmesan, herbs and the hot sauce. Season to taste with salt and pepper. Allow the mixture to cook down for a few minutes, watching closely so that it does not burn, then remove it from the heat and keep it warm.

3 Place another frying pan on the side of the coals and add the olive oil. When the oil has heated up, add the breadcrumbs and give them a stir. Let them heat through and crisp up, then remove them from the heat.

4 Set the oysters on a serving platter and carefully spoon 1 heaped teaspoon of the cheese mixture on to each, followed by a teaspoonful of the breadcrumb mixture. Using long-handled tongs, arrange the oysters directly on the hot coals. Let them cook for 5-10 minutes, or until the topping on the oysters is bubbling. Remove with tongs and serve on the platter. Sprinkle over extra chopped herbs to garnish, and serve immediately with the lemon wedges and some hot sauce.

BBQ KING
SCALLOPS

If you're planning on presenting these as a taster before the main event, place a tablespoon of creamy grits on each, and squeeze on a few veggies. They make for perfect finger food, but do let the shells cool down a little before handing them out. You can use queen scallops, but you'll need to reduce the grilling time and, without the shell, they just won't be as impressive.

SERVES 4 AS A MAIN, OR 6 AS A SMALL PLATE (2 EACH)

20g hazelnuts or pine nuts, roughly chopped

100g unsalted butter

2 tsp chopped shallot

1 tsp fresh lemon juice

1 tbsp chopped fresh coriander

1 tbsp chopped fresh parsley

12 king scallops on the half shell

12 pinches Smoked Garlic and Herb Crust (see page 23), or flaked sea salt

6 tsp chopped Chicken Skin Cracklings (see page 196)

freshly ground black pepper

1 Prepare your barbecue for direct high heat. If using coal, then you'll need a mature fire with a decent ash covering.

2 Place a dry frying pan over a medium heat. Add the chopped nuts and toast them for 4-5 minutes, or until golden. Watch the nuts closely, as they can burn very quickly. Remove from the heat and set aside.

3 Place a saucepan over a medium heat and add the butter. When it has melted, add the shallot, lemon juice, herbs and cracked pepper. (If you are using flaked salt instead of the crust, add 1 teaspoon of crushed garlic to the saucepan at this point.) Let this cook for a couple of minutes, then remove the pan from the heat and set aside.

4 Take a scallop and loosen it from its shell. Drizzle 1 teaspoon of the melted butter onto it. Repeat with the rest of the scallops. Using long-handled tongs, place the scallops in their shells directly on the coals and cook for 2 minutes. Then carefully and evenly spread a spoonful of the toasted chopped nuts on each scallop and cook for another 1½ minutes.

5 Using the tongs, carefully remove the scallops from the barbecue and place them on a platter. Sprinkle each with a pinch of the Smoked Garlic and Herb Crust (or flaked sea salt, if using) followed by half a teaspoon of Chicken Skin Cracklings and serve immediately.

BBQ SOFT SHELL CRAB S'WICH

New Orleans, which straddles the Mississippi, is famous for the quality of its soft-shell crabs and even more famous for the 'po'boy' sandwiches the crab find themselves in. Po'boys are typically made with crispy French baguettes but, to us, the bread-to-filling ratio is wrong. We prefer to maximise the filling vertically rather than horizontally, sandwiching it all with a lighter glazed bread bun. This is a decadent mixture of spicy, crunchy slaw, soft grilled sweet onions and freshly sliced tomato, with the buttery crispness of the soft shell and milky soft crabmeat.

SERVES 4

Crab butter

225g unsalted butter

4 tbsp extra virgin olive oil, plus extra for brushing

1 tsp fine sea salt

1 tsp freshly ground black pepper

4 tsp Louisiana Hot Sauce (see page 175)

juice of 2 small lemons

4 rashers smoked bacon, fried until crisp then crumbled

Slaw

60g ketchup

2 tbsp red wine vinegar

1 tbsp celery salt

1 tsp fine sea salt

¼ tsp freshly ground black pepper

⅛ tsp cayenne pepper

½ small head red cabbage, finely sliced

4 large (or 8 small) soft-shell crabs, rinsed and cleaned

1 large white onion, sliced thickly on the round

oil, for brushing

salt and freshly ground black pepper

4 glazed bread buns, halved

4 thick slices of beefsteak tomato

dash of Louisiana Hot Sauce (see page 175)

1 First, make the crab butter. Place a saucepan over a medium-low heat, add the butter and, when it has melted, add the olive oil, salt, pepper, hot sauce, lemon juice and crumbled bacon. Leave it to simmer for 2 minutes, then remove from the heat and set aside to cool.

2 Make the slaw by whisking together the ketchup, red wine vinegar, celery salt, sea salt, black pepper and cayenne in a large bowl. Add the cabbage and mix together. Cover and chill for at least 2 hours.

3 Place the cleaned crabs on a plate. Liberally coat the crabs with the butter sauce, getting right into all the crevices. Save the remaining sauce for basting. Cover the crabs and place them in the fridge to marinate for at least 2 hours.

4 Prepare your grill for direct medium heat. When it's ready, place the crabs on the grill top-side down. Baste with the remaining butter sauce while they cook. Cook the crabs for about 3-4 minutes on each side, or until they turn crisp at the edges and firm up all over.

5 Meanwhile, brush oil on the onion slices, season with salt and pepper and grill until they are partly softened and caramelised. Don't overcook them, as you want to keep a little crunch in the middle for texture.

6 Once cooked, remove the crabs and onion slices from the grill and set them aside while you toast the buns on both sides. Once toasted, it's time to build the sandwiches.

7 For each sandwich, lay a slice of tomato and some grilled onion on the bottom bun, then add 1 large (or 2 small) crabs and add a dash of hot sauce. Finish with a large spoonful of slaw and crown the whole thing with the top half of the bun. Serve immediately.

CHAPTER 4

FEASTS

CABRITO ASADO

This is a feasting recipe, and can be quite a spectacle when your guests arrive to witness a whole animal roasting near the hot embers of a fire. Cabrito is the Spanish name for the meat of a young goat. We use the asado style of roasting, which requires the use of a gridiron big enough to splay the goat. A gridiron can be made at home, but you'll need some sturdy metal poles, metal drill bits and sterile wire to secure the goat (or lamb) in place.

SERVES 10-12

13–15kg goat kid

olive oil, for rubbing into the meat

300g Cabrito Dry Rub (see page 18)

Spritz

100ml Worcestershire sauce

100ml unsweetened apple juice

300ml lager

100ml olive oil

50ml fresh lemon juice

25g fine sea salt

Suggested sides and sauces

Burnt Beets (see page 158)

Corn in the Husk (see page 162)

BBQ Greens (see page 160)

'Triple 6' Hot Sauce (see page 172)

Pickleback BBQ Sauce (see page 171)

1 Prepare the gridiron and fire (see page 241).

2 Place the goat skin-side down on a clean table and trim off any unwanted organs such as lungs or heart. You can keep the kidneys attached though.

3 Place the gridiron over the top of the goat and adjust the horizontal bars so the goat is stretched up and out as far as possible. Secure the horizontal bars in that position.

4 Grab the wire and secure the hind legs by wrapping the wire around the bottom horizontal bar and legs. Twist the two ends of the wire around each other a few times. Do the same with the front legs, ensuring the goat is fully extended.

5 To secure the middle section of the goat, pierce the wire through the skin and meat either side of the spine (trying to avoid hitting the fillet) and secure to the middle horizontal bar. You can do this more than once if you have a larger beast to cook. You may also need to secure the rump area of the goat using the same piercing technique you used for the middle.

6 Now that the gridiron is in place, massage the oil into the goat and then work the dry rub into both sides, making sure it reaches into all the nooks and crannies. Once the beast is rubbed, ask a friend to help you take it to the fire.

7 Place the gridiron into the tubing or directly into the ground near the fire, skin-side facing away from the heat. Carefully test the heat from the fire by placing your hand near the goat to see how hot it is. If you can hold your hand without burning for more than 20 seconds, you'll need to move the coals and logs closer to the gridiron. You can always move the heat further away if the meat starts catching.

8 A 13kg kid can take up to 6 hours to cook depending on how you've set the fire up, but remember to turn the beast every 30 minutes or so.

9 Once the gridiron is set up, make the spritz by adding all the ingredients to a clean and sterilised spray bottle. Shake the mixture and spritz the goat every 30 minutes from a distance so you don't burn yourself.

10 After 1 hour of cooking on each side, check the internal temperature with a digital probe thermometer. Bear in mind that you want to cook the goat to a temperature of 60°C (140°F) for medium or 65°C (150°F) for medium well. We prefer to cook whole goat to a slightly higher temperature than lamb as we like the crispy bits, especially the belly section! Don't worry too much if some of the meat looks a little blackened. It's probably just the Worcestershire sauce in the spritz.

11 When the goat is fully cooked, remove it from the fire and let it rest gridiron-side up on a clean heat-proof table (wood) covered with baking parchment. Once the gridiron has cooled, cut the wire with some pliers and set the gridiron aside.

12 Once the meat is fully rested, place your sides and sauces around the goat. This feast is great with a jug of Michelada (see page 228) or any other beer cocktail you fancy.

PIG FEAST

There are loads of ways to cook a pig, but hot-smoking with wood or roasting over a fire are arguably the best. With a few breezeblocks and some thick metal bars laced together with wire, you can re-create this cooking style in your own back garden (see page 244). Brining a larger 13-18kg 'weaner' pig (which is older than a suckling pig and has been weaned from its mother) the night before using citrus juices should feed a troop of about 20 quite easily.

SERVES 15-20

13–18kg weaner pig, split

400g Slow Pork Rub (see page 17)

North Carolina Mopping BBQ Sauce (see page 168)

10 large roasting potatoes, such as Maris Pipers, peeled and quartered

6 onions, peeled and quartered

8 carrots, halved

2 heads of garlic, cut in half

bunch of fresh rosemary

bunch of fresh oregano

200ml olive oil

sea salt and freshly ground black pepper

4 loaves white bread

Brine

3 litres warm water

freshly squeezed juice of 20 limes and 8 oranges, to make 1.5 litres in total

500g soft dark brown sugar

500g sea salt

cloves from 6 heads of garlic, finely chopped

10 dried bay leaves

10 x 2kg bags of ice cubes

1 Build your pig roaster and cage and prepare your cool box, which needs to be big enough to house the pig overnight with the lid closed (see page 244).

2 Make the brine by adding the warm water, lime and orange juice, brown sugar, sea salt, garlic and bay leaves to a very large, watertight cool box. Stir until the sugar and salt have completely dissolved. Allow the mixture to cool and then pour in the contents of 3 bags of ice to lower the temperature further.

3 Once the brine reaches 5°C (40°F), submerge the pig, weighing it down with another 2 bags of ice. If the pig is too big to be submerged, top up the container with water to cover. Close the lid of the cool box. Brine the pig overnight, topping up with more ice to keep the internal temperature of the cool box at or below 5°C (40°F).

4 The following day, make the beer mop by combining all the ingredients (see page 124) in a large saucepan over a medium heat, stir. Warm the mop gently to blend the ingredients, then remove from the heat and set aside. Remove the pig from the cool box and discard the brine. Place the pig in the pan and dry it off. Work the Slow Pork Rub into all the sides and all the crevices. Leave the pig for 30 minutes to 1 hour, or until it reaches room temperature.

5 In the meantime, in a separate barbecue, build a large charcoal fire using 16kg of lumpwood charcoal. These hot coals will be relocated into each corner of the pig roaster placed in the large tray, which will be set on top of the pig roaster to create an oven environment to help crackle the skin. Once the coals are hot, use the spade to transfer half of the coals to the pig roaster, dividing them into each of the four corners. Top up the barbecue with more coals for later use.

CONTINUED

Beer mop

2 litres IPA (see page 232) or lager

1 litre unsweetened
apple juice

500ml cider vinegar

3 tbsp freshly cracked
black peppercorns

2 tbsp English mustard powder

2 tbsp dried chilli flakes

Garlic mojo

200ml olive oil

300ml freshly squeezed lime juice
(about 12 limes)

3 tbsp finely chopped garlic

1 tsp ground cumin

120g chopped fresh oregano leaves

½ tsp salt

Suggested sides

Corn in the Husk (see page 162)

Potato Salad (see page 143)

6 Two people will be needed to move the pig into the sterilised cage. Once it is in the cage, secure it with sterilised wire and then position the pig skin-side up over the roaster. Insert a meat thermometer into the thickest part of the hind leg and place the pig tray over the pig. Transfer coals to the four corners of the pig tray, directly above the coals you placed there in step 5. Roast the pig for 3-5 hours, or until the internal temperature reaches 85°C (185°F). While it is roasting, continue to top up the 8 coal fires with a small spadeful of coal every hour or so, and baste the pig with the beer mop.

7 Combine the potatoes, onions, carrots, garlic and fresh herbs in a large roasting tin. Drizzle with the olive oil and toss everything around to coat then season with salt and pepper. Set the vegetables aside until the final hour of cooking the pig. At this point, remove the pig tray and pig from the roaster and place the tray of vegetables into the middle of the bed of the roaster. Place the pig and the pig tray back on the roaster. Leave the vegetables to cook for around 45 minutes.

8 Once the internal temperature of the meat has reached 85°C (185°F), remove the cage containing the pig from the roaster and flip the cage over so the pig is skin-side up. Score the skin with a sharp knife and baste it with the beer mop. Add more coal to the bed of the roaster, spreading the coals out evenly around the tray of vegetables. Return the pig in its cage to the roaster for a further 30-40 minutes.

9 In the meantime make the mojo. Add all of the ingredients to a bowl and blend using a hand-held stick blender (or a food processor). Once blended, cover with cling film and refrigerate until needed. Now cover the wooden picnic table with clean plastic sheeting.

10 When the pig skin is crispy, remove the cage from the roaster, unclip it and lift out the pig. Set the pig, skin-side down, on the prepared picnic table. Brush the mojo all over the meat then flip the pig over, part the crackling in places and brush the rest of the mojo into the gaps and directly on the meat.

11 Remove the vegetables from the roaster and transfer them to a serving platter. Break open the loaves of white bread, pour the North Carolina BBQ Sauce into several dipping bowls and serve the sides with the pig.

SEAFOOD BOIL

This seafood boil is to folk living in and around the Pacific regions what pig pickin' is to those living in the Carolinas. The recipe takes a little planning, and needs some big equipment, including a 10-litre stockpot and a very large colander. But, once everything is prepped and the fires are burning it won't be long until a mound of tasty seafood is poured all over your table, ready to be pounced on. We've suggested a few easily obtainable seafood varieties, but this recipe lends well to ad-libbing, so go crazy.

SERVES 10-12

1 litre water

1 litre beer

1 litre chicken stock

1 tbsp fine sea salt

1 tbsp whole black peppercorns

1 tbsp Louisiana Hot Sauce
(see page 175)

2 tbsp Old Bay-style rub (see page 20),
plus extra for sprinkling

3 dried bay leaves

1 tbsp Worcestershire sauce

6 medium waxy potatoes
(Maris Pipers are good), halved

3 whole corn on the cob, cut into thirds

500g smoked sausage, such as
kielbasa, cut into 2cm slices

1 tsp crushed dried chilli flakes

2 lemons, halved

1 large Spanish onion, peeled and cut
into wedges

3 cloves garlic, chopped

12 fresh crab claws

600g fresh clams

600g fresh razor clams

1.2kg fresh mussels, cleaned and
bearded (discard any that do not shut
when tapped on the counter top; these
are dead)

2kg prawns, deveined (whole or shelled)

To serve

125g butter, melted

juice of ½ lemon

2 tbsp chopped fresh parsley

2 tsp Old Bay-style rub (see page 20)

1 Pour the water, beer, chicken stock, salt, peppercorns, hot sauce, bay rub, bay leaves and Worcestershire sauce into a 10-litre stockpot over a high heat and bring it to the boil. Add the potatoes and boil them for 10 minutes, then add the corn and boil for a further 10 minutes. When the potatoes are soft to the touch but still a little firm, remove them, along with the corn, from the stock using a slotted spoon. Place them into a large bowl and set to one side.

2 Reduce the heat under the stockpot and let the liquid simmer while you place the sliced sausage into a large bowl and sprinkle over the crushed chillies. Mix everything together well with your hands. Press the chillies into the meat. Add the sliced sausage, lemon halves, onion and garlic to the stockpot, raise the heat to high and let it boil for 7-10 minutes.

3 When the mixture is boiling fast, add the crab claws, clams, razor clams and mussels and boil for 5 minutes. Next, add the deveined prawns. At this point, return the potatoes and corn to the pot to get hot again.

4 Meanwhile, place the butter in a small saucepan over a medium heat. When it has melted, stir in the lemon juice and parsley, and warm through.

5 When the clams and mussels have opened their shells, strain out all the liquid over the sink, using a large colander to catch all the ingredients. It is very important to discard any mussels or clams that have not opened in the cooking process. These can give you food poisoning.

6 The best way to enjoy a seafood boil is to cover your table with old newspapers and pour the contents of the colander into the centre of the table for everyone to pick at. Sprinkle the bay rub over the contents. Serve with the lemon parsley butter and some freshly baked crusty white bread to mop up the juices.

CAMPFIRE BREAKFAST FEAST
HUEVOS RANCHEROS

Have you ever woken up the morning after an evening around the campfire and needed something to restore your faith in living past 12pm? Cue Huevos Rancheros, a traditional Mexican brunch of eggs, chillies, tomatoes and tortillas. We don't know what it is about this dish, but it has magic powers beyond understanding. Be sure to use corn tortillas, and not the flour tortillas used for wraps. This is Tex-Mex at its best.

SERVES 4

25g unsalted butter

2 medium onions, diced

1 large green pepper, deseeded and diced

1 jalapeño, deseeded and diced

1 clove garlic, crushed

¼ tsp cayenne pepper

¼ tsp ground cumin

½ tsp sweet smoked paprika

¼ tsp dried oregano

400g can chopped tomatoes

200g mature Cheddar cheese, grated

2 tomatoes, diced

1 tbsp chopped fresh coriander

2 limes, cut into wedges

8 corn tortillas, left whole

sunflower oil, for frying

8 free-range eggs

hot sauce, such as Louisiana Hot Sauce (see page 175), to serve

salt and freshly ground black pepper, to taste

1 Heat the butter in a frying pan over a medium heat. Add three-quarters of the onion, then add the pepper, jalapeño and garlic and fry until the onions have turned soft. Add all dried spices and herbs to the pan and cook for 5 minutes, then pour in the chopped tomatoes, bring to a simmer and cook over a medium heat for 20 minutes. Season with salt and pepper, add the grated cheese, mix gently, then immediately remove the pan from the heat and set aside.

2 Put the rest of the onion in a bowl with the diced tomato and coriander and mix to make a salsa, then squeeze in the juice of half a lime.

3 Shallow fry the tortillas for 2 minutes on each side in 1cm-deep sunflower oil until crispy but not burnt.

4 Put another frying pan over the heat, add 150ml sunflower oil and gently fry the eggs. Place 2 corn tortillas on each plate, and top with a generous dollop of the onion, tomato and cheese mixture.

5 Add 2 fried eggs to each serving, then finish with some of the fresh tomato and onion salsa. Serve with lime wedges and some hot sauce.

CORNED BEEF HASH

In our book (pardon the pun!), BBQ is the breakfast of champions. Don't be afraid to add your own extras, such as more eggs, bacon, pulled meats, herbs or fresh chillies for a kick. This recipe makes the best of leftovers and has a South Carolina twist with some sweet mustard barbecue sauce, which matches well with the corned beef. It's a bit like a bubble and squeak recipe, but mo' better, as this one is cooked straight over hot coals in a casserole to add a slightly smokier note. The additional heat from the top of the casserole will crisp the exterior of the hash. You can, of course, use a regular kitchen hob if you don't have a campfire on the go.

SERVES 4

200g baking potatoes, peeled

2 tbsp vegetable oil

4 tbsp unsalted butter

300g smoked brisket, shredded

50g South Carolina BBQ Sauce (see page 169)

1 white onion, finely chopped

1 large green pepper, finely chopped

200g cornbread, diced

4 large eggs

50g Cheddar cheese, grated

Louisiana Hot Sauce (see page 175), to serve (optional)

fine sea salt and freshly ground black pepper

1 Grate the potatoes onto a clean tea towel and salt them lightly. Allow the salt to penetrate the potatoes for about 20 minutes while they release some moisture. This will help to really crisp the potatoes up during the cooking process.

2 After 20 minutes or so, squeeze the juice out of the potatoes by wringing the tea towel over a sink with both hands.

3 Heat the oil and half the butter in a casserole directly on the coals or in a pan over a high heat, if using a hob. Add the grated potato and stir frequently for 5 minutes or until the potato starts to brown.

4 Add the brisket and cook for about 3 minutes, stirring with a wooden spoon, until the meat releases some fat and has browned slightly. Now add the mustard BBQ sauce to the beef and cook for 2-3 minutes or until the mixture starts to stick to the pan. Stir in the onion, pepper and the cornbread and cook for about 6 minutes, undisturbed, until the mixture browns and crisps on the bottom. Continue cooking for about 15 minutes, turning the hash as it browns evenly.

5 Meanwhile, heat the remaining butter in a non-stick frying pan over a medium-high heat. Fry the eggs sunny-side up or over-easy and season with salt and pepper.

6 Place the grated cheese on top of the hash, reduce the heat and let sit for a minute until the cheese melts. To serve, top each portion of hash with a fried egg. Add a dash of Louisiana Hot Sauce if you're brave enough.

SADDLEBAG PANCAKES

These huge pancakes are filled with cooked diced bacon or sausage, and served with fried eggs for good measure. The combination of sweetness with breakfast meats is nothing new, but this dish brings together all those things we know and love from classic American breakfast menus. Drizzle with maple syrup for a truly unforgettable breakfast experience.

MAKES 8 PANCAKES

6 medium free-range eggs, plus 4 free-range eggs for frying

250ml whole milk

1 tsp vanilla extract

250g plain flour

75g caster sugar

1 tsp baking powder

vegetable oil, for frying

8 rashers smoked streaky bacon, cooked and diced, or 4 farmhouse breakfast sausages, cooked and sliced

maple syrup, for drizzling

1 Separate the six eggs into two clean mixing bowls.

2 Add the milk and vanilla to the bowl with the egg yolks and whisk. Now add the flour, sugar and baking powder, and whisk vigorously to incorporate as much air as possible and get rid of any lumps. Add the bacon or sausage to the batter.

3 Using a clean whisk, whisk the egg whites until they form soft peaks. Gently add the egg whites to batter, folding them in carefully to retain as much air as possible.

4 Put a large frying pan over a high heat and leave it to get hot. Take some kitchen paper, roll it into a ball, then pour a little vegetable oil on it. Turn the heat down to medium and carefully rub the hot pan with the oiled paper. There should be enough oil to see that the pan has been greased, but not too much or the pancake will fry, not grill.

5 Pour a portion of the batter into the hot pan so it just covers the surface thinly. Using a palette knife, carefully lift the edges of the pancake. The pancake is ready to turn when you are able to shake the pan and the pancake dislodges. Carefully turn the pancake over and cook the other side. Repeat this process until all the batter is used up, and you have a pile of pancakes.

6 Pour some more oil into the pan, turn the heat down and gently fry the eggs, making sure to baste the top of the eggs with hot oil until the whites are cooked and the yolks still runny.

7 Serve the pancakes on warm plates, top with the fried eggs and finish with a drizzle of maple syrup.

CHAPTER

5

SIDE DISHES

MAC-N-CHEESE
(WITH AN EPIC TWIST)

To make our mac-n-cheese absolutely epic, we serve it in a bacon weave bowl, but you can make it without the bowl, too. For the bowl you will need a couple of 2-litre ovenproof glass serving bowls, about 21cm in diameter, or 2 ovenproof dishes of the same shape and size. One needs to fit snugly inside of the other so it clamps the bacon in place.

SERVES 8

16 rashers thick-cut smoked streaky bacon

250g elbow macaroni

50g unsalted butter

1 small onion, grated, juices reserved

1 clove garlic, finely chopped

½ tsp ground white pepper

½ tsp sweet paprika

20g plain flour

125ml double cream, room temperature

125ml whole milk, room temperature

125g Monterey Jack cheese, grated

125g mature Cheddar cheese, grated

1 tbsp chopped fresh parsley, to garnish

salt and freshly ground black pepper

1 To make the bacon bowl, preheat the oven to 190°C/Gas 5. Take 8 pieces of the bacon and lay them horizontally on a sheet of aluminium foil, placing them closely together. From the top of the strips, fold back over just enough of every second piece of bacon, so a vertical piece of bacon can be woven through, starting from the left (see photo). Peel the top piece of horizontal bacon back to the left, so it overlaps the first piece of vertical bacon. Now lay a second vertical piece directly next to the first piece of vertically placed bacon. Fold back the turned-over horizontal pieces, to weave in the second vertically placed piece of bacon.

2 Repeat this process until all 16 rashers have been woven. Carefully drape the bacon into an ovenproof serving bowl, covering the entire bowl. Take the second bowl and set it inside of the first, pressing it down slightly. Bake for 15-20 minutes then remove it from the oven (reduce the oven temperature to 180°C/Gas 4). Leave it to cool before lifting the top bowl.

3 Bring a large pan of salted water to the boil. Add the macaroni and let it boil until well cooked - al dente is not what you are trying to achieve here. Drain the pasta in a colander. Don't worry if it clumps together.

4 While the macaroni is boiling, place a large saucepan over a medium heat and add the butter. Then add the grated onion, including the juices, and cook until just tender, stirring occasionally. Add the garlic, white pepper, paprika, and salt and pepper to taste, and simmer for a few minutes.

5 Sprinkle the flour evenly into the pan, then stir in quickly to avoid lumps. Slowly stir in the double cream and milk. Bring to a simmer, stirring occasionally, and cook the sauce for about 8 minutes, or until slightly thickened. Add 100g of the Monterey Jack cheese and 100g of the Cheddar. Stir until the cheese has melted, then take off of the heat.

6 Give the cheese mixture a good stir, pour the macaroni into the cheese and toss until thoroughly combined. Season with salt and pepper to taste, then gently pour the macaroni mixture into the bacon bowl. Sprinkle over the remaining cheese and place the dish into the oven on the top shelf. Bake for 10-15 minutes, or until the cheese on top is grilled. Garnish with chopped parsley and serve.

S L A W S

Slaws, or coleslaws, are a match made in BBQ heaven. They are typically made from thinly sliced raw cabbage and offer an awesome crunchy texture when paired with smoked meats. Unlike mayonnaise-based coleslaws, the most traditional of all slaws is the 'red' slaw, which hails from Lexington, North Carolina. This is made using ketchup and vinegar and goes perfectly in a pulled pork or smoked chicken sandwich. We tend to avoid using mayonnaise, and ketchup for that matter, in our slaws. Instead we use vinaigrette-based mixtures which add a sour tang, that helps to cut through the fat in the smoked meats we serve.

RED'S SLAW

This simple slaw recipe can be prepared well before the cook-out and, as long as you don't dress it until served, it keeps in the fridge for up to 2 days.

SERVES 8

1kg red cabbage

1 red onion

250g carrots, grated

1 large red pepper, deseeded and finely diced

10 sprigs of fresh coriander, roughly chopped

flaked sea salt and freshly cracked black pepper, to taste

Dressing

35g caster sugar

25g ready-made English mustard

60ml apple cider vinegar

250ml light olive oil

1 Make the dressing by whisking the sugar, mustard and vinegar together in a mixing bowl or jug. Slowly drizzle the oil into the bowl and whisk vigorously to combine all the ingredients. (It's best to use a small hand-held stick blender or food processor for this.) The aim is to incorporate as much air into the oil as possible in order to emulsify the dressing, which then keeps the oil from separating. Continue blending or whisking until the dressing thickens. If you feel it is too thick, whisk in a couple of tablespoons of warm water right at the end. Pour the dressing into a bowl, cover with cling film and store in the fridge until needed. If you dress the slaw too early it will make the salad limp and unappealing in appearance.

2 If you have a food processor, fit it with the finest blade you have and pass the cabbage through. Or use a sharp knife and carefully shred the cabbage as thinly as possible. For the best results, begin by cutting the cabbage into wedges and removing the core from each wedge. Then cut across the length of the wedges as thinly as possible. Add the sliced cabbage to a large bowl. Use the same process for the onion and stir it into the cabbage.

3 Stir in the carrots, pepper and toss well. Add the coriander and give it a toss to distribute it through the slaw.

4 When you are ready to dress the slaw, remove the dressing from the fridge, give it a good shake in case it has split a little when it was resting and pour it evenly over the cabbage mixture. Toss thoroughly to coat, season to taste and serve.

CITRUS AND RED CHILLI SLAW

The fresh flavours of this salad are well matched to the strong smoky tastes of barbecued meats.

SERVES 6-8

1kg red cabbage

1 red onion

1 large red pepper, deseeded and finely diced

250g carrots, grated

1–2 fresh red jalapeño peppers, deseeded and finely chopped

10 sprigs of fresh coriander, roughly chopped

flaked sea salt and freshly cracked black pepper, to taste

Dressing

35g caster sugar

25g ready-made English mustard

60ml cider vinegar

juice and grated zest of 1 lime

250ml rapeseed oil (or any oil that does not have a strong flavour)

1 Make the dressing by mixing the sugar, mustard, vinegar and lime juice in a bowl or jug. Reserve the zest for later. Drizzle in the oil, whisking the ingredients vigorously to combine. Use a small hand-held stick blender for this or a food processor. Once the dressing is thick, add the lime zest and set aside until you are ready to dress the slaw.

2 If you have a food processor, fit it with the finest blade you have and pass the cabbage through the machine. If not, use a sharp knife and carefully shred the cabbage as thinly as possible. For the best results, begin by cutting the cabbage into wedges and removing the core from each wedge. Then cut across the length of the wedges as thinly as possible. Add the sliced cabbage to a large bowl. Use the same process for the onion and stir it into the cabbage.

3 Stir in the carrots, pepper and jalapeño peppers and toss well so you have flecks of colour throughout the slaw. Add the coriander and give it a toss to distribute it through the slaw.

4 When you are ready to dress the slaw, remove the dressing from the fridge, give it a good shake in case it has split a little and pour it evenly over the cabbage mixture. Toss thoroughly to coat. Season to taste and serve.

JB'S POTATO SALAD

Potato salad is a barbecue staple, and is loved so much that it's often sold by the pint. We found that many recipes in the US were incredibly sweet, so when John Beard, one of our pitmasters, developed this different take we knew we had to put it on the menu. The soured cream and bacon balance out the flavours well, and the celery adds a really lovely crunchiness. We never get bored of eating this alongside a few slices of juicy smoked brisket (see page 48).

SERVES 10

1kg new or salad potatoes, scrubbed

150g smoked streaky bacon, diced

1 large green pepper, deseeded and finely diced

2 large sticks (about 100g) celery, finely diced

1 medium white onion, finely diced

150g good quality mayonnaise

150ml soured cream

100g wholegrain mustard

flaked sea salt and freshly ground black pepper, to taste

1 Add the potatoes to a large pan of salted water and bring to the boil. Cook until they are still firm to the touch and not overcooked. Remove from the heat, drain and refresh the potatoes under cold running water (if necessary, add them to a bowl of iced water to halt the cooking process).

2 Sauté the diced bacon in a shallow frying pan on the hob until crisp and set aside to drain.

3 Dice the cooled potatoes into 1cm cubes and put them into a large bowl. Add the pepper, celery, onion and cooked bacon and set aside. Whisk together the mayonnaise, soured cream and mustard until blended and add to the potato mixture. Stir well and season with salt and pepper to taste. Make sure that everything has a good coating of dressing. Put the salad in the fridge to chill before serving.

SALTED PRETZEL ROLLS

Like a pretzel, this bread has a salty, dark crust and a tender texture - perfect for burgers and sandwiches.

MAKES 8 ROLLS

375ml water, warmed to 43°C

7g sachet fast action
dried yeast

2 tsp caster sugar

560g plain flour,
plus extra for dusting

2 tsp salt

60g unsalted butter, melted

40g bicarbonate of soda

1 egg, lightly beaten

rock salt, for sprinkling

1 Mix the water, yeast and sugar in a bowl. Set aside to rest for 5-10 minutes, or until the yeast starts to activate and the mixture looks foamy.

2 Place the flour, salt and melted butter in a mixing bowl or the bowl of a stand mixer. Use the dough-hook attachment or electric mixer and mix at a low speed. With the machine running, slowly pour in the yeast and water mixture in a constant stream. Continue mixing until a dough forms and begins to pull away from the inside of the bowl.

3 Remove the bowl from the mixer and cover loosely with cling film or a damp tea towel. Leave the dough to rest in a warm place for 1 hour. Meanwhile, line a large baking sheet with baking parchment and set aside. After 1 hour, or when the dough has doubled in size, knock it back and turn it out onto a lightly floured work surface.

4 Cut the dough into 8 pieces, each weighing about 140g. Take one piece of dough and start forming a round ball by pulling the sides to the centre and pinching to seal. Place, pinched-side down, on a work surface and lightly roll the ball around the palm of your hand. Place seam-side down on the prepared baking sheet. Leave enough space between each roll to allow them to rise without touching. Cover as before and leave to rest in a warm place for 30 minutes, or until they rise and double in size.

5 Preheat the oven to 220°C/Gas 7 and place an oven rack in the middle. Bring 1 litre of water to a gentle boil in a large saucepan. Remove the saucepan from the heat and very slowly add the bicarbonate of soda, whisking continuously. Return the saucepan to the heat and to simmer.

6 Poach the buns by placing 2 or 3 at a time into the liquid, seam-side down. Poach for 30 seconds, then carefully turn over and poach for another 30 seconds. Remove them with a slotted spoon and return to the prepared baking sheet, seam-side down. Repeat with the remaining rolls.

7 Using a pastry brush, brush each roll with the beaten egg, making sure to coat all sides completely. Sprinkle each roll with a little rock salt then, using a sharp straight-edged knife, cut an 'X' in the top.

8 Bake the rolls in the oven for 15-20 minutes. Remove from the oven and transfer to a cooling rack.

SOURDOUGH STARTER

Making a sourdough starter takes about six days, depending on the conditions in your kitchen. Each day you 'feed' the starter with equal amounts of fresh flour and water. As long as you see bubbles and signs of yeast activity each day, continue feeding it regularly. After about six days you'll have a starter that can be maintained for weeks and months, giving you the ability to bake fresh sourdough bread as and when you need it.

MAKES 1 LOAF

350g strong plain white flour

350ml spring water

DAY 1: MAKING THE STARTER

1 Place 70g of the flour and 70ml warmed spring water in a 1-litre glass or plastic container with a lid. Mix vigorously until combined into a smooth paste. Scrape down the sides of the container and then loosely cover with the lid, but leave it open a little to allow the yeasts to breathe.

2 Place somewhere with a consistent room temperature of around 21°C (70°F), and out of direct sunlight. Leave it undisturbed for 24 hours.

DAYS 2-5: FEEDING THE STARTER

1 You should see a few bubbles working their way to the top of your starter. This is good! It means that yeasts have started to eat the sugars in the flour and release carbon dioxide and alcohol, which helps fight any bacteria that might be present. If you don't have bubbles after 24 hours, you may have to move the starter to a warmer place in your kitchen.

2 Measure out another 70g flour and 70ml warmed spring water and mix them into the starter in the container. Scrape the sides clean again, and loosely place the lid back on the container. Repeat this process every 24 hours for 3 more days.

DAY 6: USING THE STARTER

1 By now, the starter should be looking very bubbly, and will have expanded into its contained home. If you stir the starter, it should feel loose and look completely webbed with bubbles. It will also smell quite sour and pungent, and even taste sour and vinegary.

2 If everything is looking, smelling, and tasting good, you can consider your starter ripe and ready to use. If your starter is lagging behind a bit, continue feeding it for another day or two. Once your starter is ready you no longer need to bulk it up.

MAINTAINING THE STARTER

To maintain the starter, use or give away about half of the starter and then 'feed' the remaining starter with new flour and water for 5 days, as you did when growing it. You should now have a constant supply of starter.

A good starter can be frozen to prolong its lifespan. If you need a break or if you are going away for an extended period, just store it in the freezer in freezer bags, with 1 or 2 cups of the starter per bag. It won't freeze completely and you won't need to feed it until you're ready to use it. If you store it in the fridge, you will need to feed it weekly, though not as often as if it were on your kitchen counter. When you feel ready to bake, just pull the bag out of the freezer or fridge and let it come to room temperature on your kitchen counter. Give it a good feed again if you want to have some starter left over. Take out what you need for the loaf and start baking.

SOURDOUGH RYE BREAD

MAKES 1 LOAF

Starter

100g rye flour

50g strong white flour

150ml water

100g Sourdough Starter
(see page 146)

Loaf

125g rye flour

125g strong white flour,
plus extra for dusting

1 tbsp caster sugar

1 tbsp caraway seeds

2 tsp salt

1 tbsp olive oil, plus extra for
oiling the bowl and the baking
sheet

4 tbsp water

100ml milk, for glazing

1 The day before you want to bake, make the rye sourdough starter. Add the rye flour, the strong white flour and the measured water to the sourdough starter. Mix these well into a batter, and put it into a plastic or glass container. Loosely cover with a lid, or cling film, set in a warm place in your kitchen and leave undisturbed for 24 hours.

2 The next day, mix the flours, sugar, caraway seeds and 1 teaspoon salt in a large mixing bowl, and make a well in the middle. Pour in the oil and measured water, and then add 250g of the starter to the well. Using a fork, stir the flour into the centre of the well to start forming a dough.

3 When it gets too difficult to use the fork, start working the dough with your hands until the dough is smooth, and comes cleanly away from the inside of the bowl. (You might need to add a little more flour to the dough to get to this consistency.)

4 Knead the dough for 2 minutes, by stretching it and then rolling it back into a ball a few times, then shape it into a ball. Oil the inside of a large bowl and place the dough into it. Oil the dough lightly, cover loosely with a damp tea towel, and put in a warm place for 30 minutes to 1 hour until it rises and doubles in size.

5 Lightly flour a clean work surface and oil a baking sheet. Place the dough on the surface and knock it back. Then knead it into a dough ball again. Shape the dough into a bloomer-shaped loaf, and put it on a greased baking sheet. Use the tip of a sharp knife to score some diagonal lines down the length of the loaf. Cover it again with a damp tea towel, and set it in a warm area for 30 minutes or so to rise until it doubles in size again. Just before you are ready to bake, preheat your oven to 180°C/Gas 4.

6 Bake for 20 minutes, or until the bread has risen and a good crust has formed, so that when you take it out to apply the glaze, it does not sink.

7 While the bread is baking, mix together the remaining salt with the milk. Remove the loaf from the oven and brush on the glaze. Return the loaf to the oven and bake for a further 25 minutes. You'll know when the loaf is ready when you thump it on the underside, and it has a hollow sound. Cool the loaf on a wire rack.

HUSH PUPPIES

This Southern soul classic owes its existence to the ingeniously varied ways the first Americans found to use maize. According to one story, the name can be attributed to hunters who used to give pieces of deep-fried leftover cornmeal to their hounds while out hunting to hush them up! We've added jalapeños and sweetcorn to this recipe to make it a side dish that will definitely hush up your mates while they motor through them.

SERVES 6-8

300g can sweetcorn, drained

125g coarse, quick-cook polenta

250g self-raising flour

½ tsp garlic powder

1 tsp baking powder

½ tsp cayenne pepper

1 tsp caster sugar

½ tsp salt

1 tsp freshly ground black pepper

1 small onion, finely diced

2 fresh green or red jalapeño peppers, deseeded and finely diced

1 egg

250ml whole milk

500ml vegetable or sunflower oil, for deep-frying

1 Divide the sweetcorn into two 150g piles. Set one pile aside, and chop up the kernels of the other pile until they resemble creamed corn. Set aside.

2 Combine all the dry ingredients, including salt and pepper, in a bowl and stir together well. Add the chopped corn, whole corn, onion and jalapeño peppers and mix well. Add the egg and then the milk. Stir everything together well to form a batter and then leave it to stand undisturbed for 10 minutes to allow it to rise.

3 While the batter is rising, heat the vegetable or sunflower oil in a deep-fryer to 175°C (347°F). Use a tablespoon to scoop out rounded balls of the batter, and carefully drop each one into the hot oil. When the hush puppies rise to the top, turn them over in the oil using long-handled tongs to cook evenly. Keep turning them until they are golden brown all over.

4 Remove the hush puppies from the hot oil using a slotted spoon and put them on a plate lined with kitchen paper to soak up any excess oil before serving.

PUMPKIN CORNBREAD

We came across this while on one of our many road trips around America. We were so impressed with this cornbread that we humbly asked the pitmaster of The Pit in Raleigh, North Carolina, for his recipe. He bakes his in a 15cm iron skillet, but this recipe can easily be baked in a muffin tin. Served with a decadent knob of maple syrup butter, you will be excused if you feel you are eating something that goes just as well with a morning cup of coffee, as with some vinegary Pulled Pork (see page 36).

SERVES 6-8

1 large pumpkin, peeled, deseeded and cubed

cooking oil spray

170g caster sugar

3 eggs, lightly beaten

300ml buttermilk

350g coarse, quick-cook polenta

300g plain flour

¾ tsp salt

1½ tsp bicarbonate of soda

1½ tsp baking powder

2 pinches ground cinnamon

1 pinch ground nutmeg

125g unsalted butter, melted

1 First, make the pumpkin purée. Put the pumpkin cubes into a large saucepan over a medium heat and add water to cover. Cook the pumpkin for 20 minutes, or until the cubes are tender. When the cubes are cooked, drain off the water and leave the cubes to cool for at least 10 minutes in a colander. When it is cool and dry, purée the pumpkin until smooth in a food processor or by hand using a masher. Any purée you do not use in the cornbread can be frozen and used for any other pumpkin recipe.

2 To make the cornbread, preheat the oven to 180°C/Gas 4. Spray a 12-hole muffin tin with cooking oil and set aside. Place the sugar, eggs, buttermilk and 250g of the pumpkin purée in a medium bowl. Beat until well blended, and set aside.

3 Place the polenta, flour, salt, bicarbonate of soda, baking powder, cinnamon and nutmeg into a large bowl and mix together well. Pour the wet ingredients into the dry mixture and stir. Add the melted butter and stir until thoroughly combined.

4 Spoon the batter into the muffin tin so that each hole is about two-thirds full. To ensure you get a good even rise out of the cornbread, slam the muffin tin down on the kitchen counter several times to release any air bubbles. Bake for 20-25 minutes, turning the pan 180 degrees after the first 10 minutes so the muffins will bake evenly.

5 The muffins are done when a wooden cocktail stick inserted into the centre comes out clean and the tops are set. Serve the muffins warm with a dollop of maple syrup butter, which is simply softened salted butter, blended with maple syrup to taste.

PIT BEANS

In the restaurant, our pit beans are made at the end of a busy service. All the little burnt ends, not-so-perfect slices of brisket and leftover pulled pork are mixed together in a roasting tray with spices and beans, then the tray is placed at the bottom of the smoker overnight.

Ideally this dish needs to be made simultaneously with primal cuts of meat and things that you are going to smoke for more than a few hours. However, because this is a greatly reduced portion, it will fare well in a smoker with just about anything. If your smoker has a water bath, we suggest placing the beans in a casserole or ovenproof dish and setting it into the water bath. Add just enough water to come up to a couple of centimetres under the rim of the dish.

SERVES 8

50g unsalted butter

1 medium white onion,
finely diced

5 cloves garlic, finely chopped

500g burnt ends, or any leftover
smoked BBQ meat

415g can kidney beans

415g can baked beans

1 tsp ground cumin

2 tsp smoked hot paprika

½ tsp cayenne pepper, or more
if you like it hot

1 tsp salt

½ tsp freshly ground black pepper

180g Kansas City-Style BBQ Sauce
(see page 174)

1 Place the butter in a very large frying pan over a low heat. Add the onion and garlic and fry them until the onion is soft and translucent. Chuck in your titbits of meat and get some heat into them, especially if they have come out of the fridge.

2 Drain the liquid off the canned kidney beans and add them to the pan, along with the can of baked beans.

3 Add the dried spices, salt and pepper, as well as the BBQ sauce. Give it all a good stir and taste for spiciness and seasoning. Pour the bean mixture into an ovenproof dish or casserole that will fit on a lower shelf of your smoker.

4 Let the beans smoke underneath your pork butt (see page 36), brisket (see page 48) or even St. Louis cut ribs (see page 32), and check on them every hour or so. If it looks like they are drying up a little, add a glug of whatever liquid you deem worthy enough (water or beer) and mix through.

5 In the restaurant, we smoke a large batch of pit beans for about 12 hours underneath our pork butts. You'll know when they are ready when the red hues from the BBQ sauce and baked bean tomato sauce have turned brown, all the liquid has evaporated and the tops of the beans begin to roast. For smaller batches, 2-4 hours should do it.

SMOKED HASSELBACKS

Hasselback potatoes are super-crunchy smoke-baked potatoes that have been fanned out using a nifty slicing trick, packed with extra ingredients and topped with soured cream, fresh red chilli slices and spring onions. If you prefer, you can also roast these in a regular oven at 220°C/Gas 7 for 50 minutes to 1 hour.

SERVES 4

4 baking potatoes, scrubbed

60g freshly grated Parmesan

120g fine breadcrumbs

5 tbsp melted unsalted butter

1 tsp smoked sweet paprika

100ml soured cream

1 fresh red chilli, thinly sliced

2 spring onions, thinly sliced

flaked sea salt and freshly cracked black pepper, to taste

WOOD

2 chunks of oak or apple wood (or any fruit hardwood) soaked in water overnight or for at least 2 hours

1 Prepare your grill for indirect smoking between 108°C (225°F) and 135°C (275°F).

2 Insert a thin metal skewer along the length of a potato, about 1cm from the bottom. Place the potato on a cutting board and hold the skewer with one hand so the skewer is parallel with the board. Using a sharp knife, cut slim slices into the potato, stopping when the knife hits the metal skewer. Remove the skewer and repeat with the other potatoes.

3 After you finish cutting each potato, hold it under cold running water as you gently flex the potato sections open, to rid the potatoes of any excess starch. Dry the potatoes well before smoking them.

4 Place the Parmesan, breadcrumbs, 1 tablespoon of the melted butter and the paprika in a food processor and add salt and pepper to taste. Process the mixture until blended. Now take 2 more tablespoons of the melted butter and use it to brush the fanned potatoes all over, making sure some gets into and between the slices. Pat the Parmesan mixture on top of each potato.

5 Add a few wood chunks to the coals to develop a smoky environment. Place the potatoes in an oiled baking tray, cover with aluminium foil and place in the smoker.

6 After 20 minutes, remove the foil and leave the potatoes to smoke for another 20 minutes, or until they turn crispy and the flesh is soft. When the internal temperature of the potatoes hits approximately 95°C (200°F), they are done.

7 Remove the potatoes from the smoker and drizzle the remaining 2 tablespoons of melted butter over. Top each potato with a tablespoon of soured cream and sprinkle of chilli and spring onions to serve.

BURNT BEETS

Roasting beetroots in the embers of a fire imbues them with an earthy, smoky flavour. Incorporating some of the resulting char in the end dish adds a mercurial depth to the flavour mix that plays beautifully with a glass of crisp Sauvignon Blanc. The soured cream dipper offers a cool temperature and texture contrast for the palate. You can also mix the charred beets with feta cheese, walnuts, peppery rocket and a light vinaigrette to create a mega-tasty, healthy salad.

SERVES 4

1kg raw beetroots, trimmed and scrubbed

1 tbsp olive oil

1 tbsp flaked sea salt, plus extra for seasoning

freshly cracked black pepper

Dipper

60ml soured cream

2 tbsp finely chopped chives

1 Prepare your barbecue with a charcoal fire and allow it to burn down to glowing embers. Meanwhile, rub the beetroots with olive oil until they develop a thin sheen, and sprinkle a generous pinch of sea salt over each one.

2 When the barbecue is ready, bury the beetroots directly into the hot coals and roast for 1-1½ hours, or until they are tender all the way through when pierced with a sharp knife. Remove them from the coals with long-handled tongs and leave them to cool. Meanwhile, mix together the soured cream and chives in a bowl and keep this in the fridge until needed.

3 Once the beetroots are cool enough to touch, slip them out of their skins, but reserve some of the charred bits. To add extra flavour and texture, finely chop one of the burnt beetroot skins with a sharp knife and mix it into the soured cream dipper. Season to taste. Cut the beetroots into wedges and serve alongside the dipper.

BARBECUE GREENS

Who said this book is all about meat? Here's a take on the widely popular dish of collard greens, found in abundance in the States but, unfortunately, a little more difficult to get your hands on here in the UK. For a Red's take we've used spring greens, so all is not lost. All too often in our experience, this large leafy vegetable is overcooked and bitter. However, one fine day in Dallas, Texas, during a pilgrimage tour, we were fortunate enough to eat in the fabulous Pecan Lodge, where Dianne Fourton served us up the most delicious example we've had to date. All that bitterness needs is a little sugar. Simple!

SERVES 6

1.5kg spring greens or turnip greens, leaves washed and trimmed (stems removed)

50g unsalted butter

1 medium white onion, finely diced

1 clove garlic, crushed

500g smoked bacon lardons, or trimmings from any of our bacon recipes, chopped

500ml water

½ tsp salt

½ tsp freshly ground black pepper

½ tsp caster sugar

chilled butter, to serve

1 Put the leaves into a large saucepan over a medium heat and cover with water. Bring the water to a simmer, drain the greens and set them aside. Set the saucepan back over the heat.

2 Add the butter, onion, garlic and bacon lardons or trimmings to the pan and gently fry until the bacon is a lovely golden colour and the fat has started to render. Now add the precooked greens and the water, turn up the heat and bring to the boil.

3 Turn the heat down and, once the water is simmering gently, cover the pan with a lid and cook for 40 minutes to 1 hour, or until the greens are tender. Season the greens with the salt, pepper and sugar, giving them a little stir to dissolve the sugar. Serve hot with a knob of chilled butter.

CORN IN THE HUSK

Grilling corn over flames gives the kernels a mellow toasty flavour that makes each ear the perfect recipient for flavoured butters and barbecue sauces. Soaking the ears of corn in water, still in their husks, before grilling steams the corn and stops the husks burning, and brushing the soaked ears with fat before they go on the grate promotes caramelisation and prevents burning.

SERVES 4

4 ears of corn, husks intact

vegetable or olive oil, for brushing

Smoky lime butter

125g unsalted butter, softened

juice of 1 lime

2 tbsp chopped fresh coriander leaves

½ tsp flaked sea salt

½ tsp smoked sweet paprika

¼ tsp fresh cracked black pepper

1 tsp honey

1 fresh red chilli, thinly sliced,
for garnishing

Herby goat's cheese butter

90g unsalted butter, softened

70g goat's cheese

2 tbsp herbes de Provence

2 cloves garlic, finely chopped

1 tsp grated lemon zest

flaked sea salt and freshly ground
black pepper, to taste

BBQ butter

90g unsalted butter, softened

3 tbsp Kansas City BBQ Sauce (see page 174), or your favourite ready-made sauce

1 Prepare your grill for high indirect cooking. Peel back the husks, leaving them attached at the base of the ear. Remove and discard the silk and pull the husks back over the corn. Place the ears in a large bowl of cold water, let them soak for 30 minutes, then drain. Brush the corn kernels with some vegetable or olive oil.

2 Oil the grill grate and place it on the grill. Arrange the ears on the grill, cover with the lid and cook for 15-20 minutes, turning them occasionally using long-handled tongs. When the husks are slightly charred, the corn is done.

3 Remove the corn from the grill and, holding the bottom of the hot ears with a towel, carefully peel back the husks. If you're adding one of the variations, left, mix all the ingredients in a bowl until smooth. Keep cool.

4 Coat the kernels with your compound butter, baste or sauce of choice. Return the corn to the grill for another 5 minutes to crisp the kernels up. Brush with more butter, baste or sauce while turning the ear 3 or 4 times. Once cooked, peel the husks back over the corn and serve.

SOUTHERN-STYLE GRITS WITH THYME AND SMOKED GARLIC

American inventiveness created another great barbecue staple using the mighty maize, and it's called grits. At Red's we've added smoked garlic and thyme to give this smacker of a classic a pouting kiss. To make smoked garlic purée, simply place a whole bulb of garlic into your smoker and leave until the garlic cloves start to soften. Squeeze out the garlic, cover with high-quality olive oil and keep sealed in a plastic tub in the fridge until needed. For this recipe it is important to use a heavy-based saucepan, as a saucepan with a thin base will cause the grits to burn.

SERVES 2

50g unsalted butter

1 tsp smoked garlic purée

2 sprigs fresh thyme, leaves picked

10g vegetable stock cube or 1 tbsp vegetable stock powder

250ml boiling water

1 tsp salt

250ml whole milk

200g coarse, quick cook polenta

½ tsp smoked paprika

8 x 1cm cubes of chilled butter

½ tsp white pepper

1 Place the butter in a heavy-based saucepan over a low-medium heat. Add the garlic purée and thyme and fry gently to release all those flavoursome oils. Meanwhile, dissolve the vegetable stock cube or powder in the boiled water, add the salt and add it to the pan. Now add the milk, turn up the heat and bring the liquid to the boil.

2 Once the liquid is boiling, turn down the heat and slowly pour the polenta into the saucepan. Stir continuously with a whisk, making sure there are no lumps. Continue to stir the grits while simmering over a low heat for about 10 minutes, or until the polenta resembles smooth porridge. If it feels too stiff, add some more liquid until you get the desired texture.

3 Put the finished grits into a serving bowl, sprinkle with the smoked paprika, and scatter over a few cubes of butter. Serve hot. If you leave it to stand for too long and it cools, it thickens and becomes less palatable. If you want to make this side dish ahead, you can always reheat it in a clean saucepan over a low heat. Make sure you add a little water and milk to loosen it. Reheat gently, stirring all the time. Season to taste.

CHAPTER

6

SAUCES AND PICKLES

NORTH CAROLINA MOPPING BBQ SAUCE

There are lots of different BBQ sauces and mops in the Carolinas. This one is vibrant red in colour, because of the tomato ketchup, but still has a devilish piquant tang.

MAKES APPROXIMATELY 400G

125g soft light brown sugar

250ml cider vinegar

50g ketchup

1 tsp Louisiana Hot Sauce
(see page 175) or your favourite
shop-bought hot sauce

½ tsp dried chilli flakes

1 scotch bonnet or habañero chilli,
cut in half

sea salt and freshly ground black
pepper, to taste

1 Warm the sugar and vinegar in a saucepan over a low heat and stir until the sugar dissolves.

2 Add the ketchup and hot sauce, and stir to blend. Taste for seasoning, then remove the pan from the heat. Let the sauce cool slightly before pouring it into a sterilised bottle with a removable lidded pouring spout.

3 Add the chilli flakes and fresh chilli for an extra kick and seal with the spout. Before serving, be sure to shake the sauce well, as the chilli flakes and fresh chilli do tend to sink to the bottom.

4 The longer you leave the fresh chilli in the vinegar, the spicier it will become. Keep checking the sauce, and remove the chilli when you have reached your heat limit. The sauce keeps for up to 2 months in the fridge.

SOUTH CAROLINA BBQ SAUCE

Take a trip south in the US, and you hit the 'Mustard Belt'. This name harks back to the early German immigrants who first settled in this area and brought their mustard-based sauces with them. Locally, mustard is known as Carolina Gold and you'll soon see why, when that sweet, spicy and tangy wave mixes with smoky Pulled Pork (see page 36) in your mouth.

MAKES APPROXIMATELY 500G

1 tsp celery seeds

1 tsp dried rosemary

60ml cider vinegar

50ml unsweetened apple juice

50ml water

125g soft light brown sugar

125g yellow American mustard

125g prepared English mustard

2 tsp Worcestershire sauce

2 tsp fresh lemon juice

½ tsp cayenne pepper

1 Grind the celery seeds and rosemary in a pestle and mortar as finely as possible. Set aside.

2 Warm the cider vinegar, apple juice, water and sugar in a saucepan over a low heat and stir continuously until the sugar dissolves. Now add the crushed celery seeds and rosemary.

3 Throw in the remaining ingredients and leave the sauce to simmer for 10 minutes, allowing it to reduce slightly so it thickens a little.

4 Remove the sauce from the heat. Let it cool slightly before pouring it into a sterilised bottle with a lid. Because of its high sugar content, this sauce will keep for up to 1 month in the fridge.

MELLOW *YELLOW* AMERICAN MUSTARD

Perhaps the best known brand of yellow American mustard is the iconic French's, first introduced at the St. Louis World Fair in 1904. You don't need us to tell you how well it goes with burgers and hot dogs, but we can show you how to make your own all-American mustard to give you added props at your BBQ party. It's easy to make and will be at its best after a week or so, but can be used immediately.

MAKES APPROXIMATELY 500G

250g ground yellow mustard

1 tsp ground turmeric

¼ tsp ground allspice

¼ tsp ground ginger

½ tsp sweet smoked paprika

2 tsp salt

1 tsp garlic powder

½ tsp onion powder

1 tsp plain flour

250ml water

175ml cider vinegar

cayenne pepper (optional)

juice of ½ fresh lemon

1 Put all the ingredients, except the cayenne and lemon juice, in a saucepan, place the pan over a medium heat and bring to the boil slowly. Using a whisk, combine all the ingredients until you have a smooth mixture.

2 Once the mixture starts to boil, reduce the heat and let the sauce simmer for 10 minutes. Remove the pan from the heat and leave the sauce to cool for a while. Taste for spiciness and add a little cayenne at this stage, if desired.

3 Tip the sauce into a food processor and blitz for 1-2 minutes, or use a hand-held stick blender. Add the lemon juice while processing - this will help to smooth out the mixture. Don't worry if it's a little grainy as it will become smoother as it matures.

4 Transfer the mustard to a sterilised jar or bottle, seal and store it in the fridge. It keeps for up to 1 month.

PICKLEBACK BBQ SAUCE

The only thing to top the partnership of BBQ and beer is BBQ, beer and bourbon. This sauce was inspired by our tour of the Wild Turkey distillery in Kentucky and our love of the pickleback - a shot of bourbon chased with a shot of pickle juice (see page 228). Kentucky is known for its mutton, which has a strong flavour, so this sauce will punch through with its heady mix of pickle, chocolate, espresso and bourbon. We suggest you keep this one just for the adults, as the alcohol doesn't burn off during preparation.

MAKES APPROXIMATELY 1 LITRE

2 tbsp olive oil

1 onion, finely diced

6 cloves garlic, roughly chopped

1 tbsp ground cumin

½ tsp dried chilli flakes

2 tsp fine sea salt

60ml brewed espresso or 1 tsp instant espresso powder

125ml pickled cucumber vinegar

60ml Wild Turkey 81, or your favourite bourbon

500g ketchup

375g soft dark brown sugar

3 wedges chocolate orange

1 Heat the olive oil in a saucepan over a medium heat. Add the onion, garlic, cumin, chilli flakes and salt and cook gently for about 10 minutes, stirring frequently, until the onion is soft and translucent. Do not allow the garlic to brown, as the burnt flavour will not work with this sauce.

2 Add the espresso, vinegar and bourbon and bring to a boil. Remove from the heat and pour the mixture into a blender. Blend on high until smooth, then return the mixture to the pan. Whisk in the ketchup and brown sugar until fully incorporated and smooth.

3 Finally, remove the pan from the heat and add the chocolate orange but do not stir. The residual heat will melt the chocolate. Leave the sauce to sit for 10 minutes, then stir to incorporate the chocolate, and serve.

4 To store, pour the sauce into a sterilised jar or bottle, and seal. It will keep in the fridge for up to 1 month.

'TRIPLE 6'
═══ HOT SAUCE ═══

We love adding a hot kick to our food, and you've only got to walk down the supermarket aisles to see that spicy sauce is big business. Our own house-made 'Triple 6' table sauce was inspired by a trip to Louisiana - home of hot sauces - but ours has a fruity twist and a few extra chillies chucked in to step it up a level. Freezing your chillies beforehand brings out more flavour. This sauce goes perfectly with chicken wings, transforming them into a fiery plate of hot deliciousness.

MAKES APPROXIMATELY 500G

2 tbsp olive oil

8 frozen chillies (extremely hot ones such as ghost, scotch bonnet, bird's-eye or habañero), defrosted

2 fresh red jalapeño peppers, roughly chopped

4 cloves garlic

227g can peach halves in syrup

227g can pineapple chunks in syrup

410g can apricot halves, drained

2 large carrots

200ml cider vinegar

25ml fresh lime juice

2 tbsp cayenne pepper

fine sea salt, to taste

1 Heat the olive oil in a large pan over a low heat. Add the whole chillies, chopped jalapeños and garlic and cook gently for 3-5 minutes or until softened. Don't let them caramelise or brown.

2 Add all the canned fruit along with the syrup from the peaches and pineapple and give it a stir. Don't add the liquid from the apricots as it would make the sauce too watery.

3 Grate the carrots straight into the pan. These will help give the sauce a vibrant colour, but the chillies you use will determine the final colour.

4 Next, add the vinegar and lime juice and bring the mixture to a simmer for 10-15 minutes or until the carrot is fully softened.

5 Take the pan off the heat and add salt to taste. Tip the sauce into a food processor and whizz for 1-2 minutes until smooth, or use a hand-held stick blender. Pour the sauce into an airtight jar or bottle. The sauce will keep for a couple of weeks in the fridge.

JUDAS KETCHUP

Ketchup is hardly a traditional BBQ sauce, but it's still an essential condiment to any good feast. In its purest form, without any added sweetness and tanginess, it somehow just doesn't work with BBQ, but this version is a little spicier. If you can get sun-ripened organic tomatoes, they will work best. Shop-bought tomatoes just won't have the flavour you're looking for.

MAKES APPROXIMATELY 1 LITRE

1 tbsp olive oil

1 large white or Spanish onion, diced

4 cloves garlic, roughly chopped

1 large red pepper, deseeded and roughly chopped

2kg sun-ripened organic tomatoes, chopped, or 2 x 410g tins chopped plum tomatoes

1 tsp cayenne pepper

½ tsp ground allspice

6 whole cloves

½ tsp black mustard seeds

½ tsp celery salt

2 tsp freshly ground black pepper

2 tsp fine sea salt

250ml red wine vinegar

250g soft light brown sugar

1 tbsp tomato purée

pinch of freshly grated nutmeg

1 Heat the olive oil in a saucepan over a low heat, and add the onion, garlic and red pepper. Let them sweat down until they have softened. Add the tomatoes - skin, seeds and all - warm them through, then add the cayenne pepper, allspice, cloves, mustard seeds, celery salt, black pepper and salt. Stir well, and simmer for 2 minutes to help infuse the flavours.

2 Add the red wine vinegar, reduce the heat, and cover the saucepan with a lid. Allow the sauce to simmer for 15 minutes.

3 Next, you need to remove the tomato seeds to make a smooth sauce and there are two ways to do this. You can blitz the sauce in a food processor or blender, then pass it through a fine-mesh sieve. Or, and this is our preferred method, pass the sauce through an old-fashioned, but more gentle, hand-cranked food mill. This does not break up the seeds and skin, which make the sauce more bitter than desired. Whichever method you choose to use, the goal is to separate the seeds, skin and any other granules and make a silky smooth sauce.

4 Pour the smooth sauce into a saucepan, place over a medium heat, and add the sugar, tomato purée and nutmeg. Leave to simmer for 15 minutes, or until the sugar and tomato paste have dissolved and cooked through. Keep stirring now and again to prevent any burning on the base of the pan. Taste for seasoning, tanginess and spiciness, and adjust if needed.

5 Remove the sauce from the heat and let it cool slightly before transferring it to a sterilised jar or bottle and sealing it with a lid. The sauce will keep in the fridge for up to 1 month.

KANSAS CITY BBQ SAUCE

Tomato-based, with a sweet, smoky flavour, is what we have to come to expect of BBQ sauce, and most shop-bought sauces are derived from this modern Kansas City style of sauce. In the past, though, barbecue in this part of America would have been served with a vinegary hot sauce, similar to the one served at Arthur Bryant's barbecue restaurant in Kansas City today. You'll need to sterilise enough jars or bottles (see page 13) to store 1 litre of the sauce, so get those ready before you start.

MAKES APPROXIMATELY 1 LITRE

1 tsp cayenne pepper

1 tsp cracked black peppercorns

2 tsp onion powder

1 tbsp garlic powder

60g smoked paprika

1 tsp salt

500g ketchup

100g Mellow Yellow American Mustard (see page 170)

125ml cider vinegar

20ml Worcestershire sauce

90g molasses

90g soft dark brown sugar

15g butter

1 medium onion, diced

1 In a small bowl, mix the cayenne, black pepper, onion powder, garlic powder, smoked paprika and salt together. In a separate bowl, mix together the ketchup, mustard, vinegar, Worcestershire sauce, molasses and brown sugar.

2 Melt the butter in a large saucepan over a low heat. Add the onion and cook for about 5 minutes until soft and translucent.

3 Add all the dry spices to the pan and stir for about 2 minutes. Then add the wet ingredients and simmer for 15 minutes over a medium heat, or until the mixture reduces and thickens.

4 You can strain the sauce if you don't want the chunks of onion, or use a hand-held stick blender to blitz until smooth.

5 The sauce can be served straight away, but it is better once cooled. It will keep in the fridge for up to 1 month in sterilised and sealed bottles or jars.

LOUISIANA HOT SAUCE

Louisiana isn't known for its barbecue, but it does have some great sauces that work well with it. This style of hot sauce is very popular across the whole state (and the world for that matter), and works particularly well with shellfish and oysters.

MAKES 500G

250ml Hot Sauce Pepper Mash
(see page 176)

1 clove garlic, cut in half

1 tsp finely chopped fresh basil

1 tsp finely chopped fresh oregano

¼ tsp ground celery seed

1 tsp freshly ground black pepper

250ml distilled white vinegar

1 Combine all the ingredients in a blender and purée. Pour the mixture through a sieve into a bowl, pushing against the mesh with a metal spoon to extract as much pepper flesh as possible. Make sure you scrape the underside of the sieve, too.

2 Discard the skins and residue left behind in the sieve.

3 Decant the sauce into sterilised bottles or jars with a removable lidded pourer attachment. Don't forget to date the bottle, and while you're at it, write a name for your sauce on the label as well. Seal the bottles and store in the fridge for up to 3 months.

JALAPEÑO-LIME HOT SAUCE

This hot sauce has a tart and spicy flavour that's highly addictive, and offers a refreshing contrasting note that works well with barbecued fish, Nacho Pie (see page 60) and Bloody Marys (see page 225).

MAKES 200G

80ml fresh lime juice

3 large green jalapeño peppers, deseeded

1 tbsp Hot Sauce Pepper Mash
(see page 176)

¼ tsp fine sea salt

2 tbsp distilled white vinegar

¼ tsp ground cumin

¼ tsp garlic powder

1 Combine all of the ingredients in a blender and purée until smooth.

2 Pour the mixture into a sterilised preserving jar. Seal and store in the fridge for up to 1 month. Make sure you give the sauce a good shake before using.

HOT SAUCE
PEPPER MASH

The secret to any serious hot sauce is a pepper mash, which forms the base of nearly all our Hot Sauces. It does take some patience to create your own, but once you've perfected it, you'll be able to create some awesome home-made hot sauces that will test even the most adventurous of palates!

MAKES APPROXIMATELY 1 LITRE

2kg fresh hot red chilli peppers, such as habañero, Thai, cayenne or scotch bonnet

60g fine sea salt

250ml spring water or cool boiled water

2 tbsp sherry vinegar

1 Wash the chillies and place them outdoors for 1-2 days, or until they are ripe and wrinkly. It's best if it's sunny but, if not, just set the chillies outside somewhere under cover.

2 Put gloves on before handling the chillies, to protect your eyes and other sensitive parts if you happen to touch them after touching the chillies. Remove the stalks from the chillies and slice them in half lengthways. Put the chillies into a large heavy bowl, sprinkle evenly with the salt and mash them gently with a potato masher. Try to keep them whole so the seeds can be removed easily later. Leave the bowl uncovered and allow the chillies to steep in their own juices overnight.

3 The following day, place the chillies and resulting juices into a large, sterilised narrow-neck preserving jar with a two-part canning lid. Add the water, making sure the jar is no more than five-eighths full, and seal loosely with the sterilised lid in order to allow for fermentation overflow. Set aside in a cool area away from direct sunlight for 2 weeks.

4 During the first week, the pepper mash should begin bubbling vigorously as a result of a fermentation process. The gas bubbles will cause the pulp in the mash to rise, leaving the liquid and some solids on the bottom. Once the bubbling starts, stir the mash down with a clean spoon every day. If it seems about to overflow, pour part of the mixture into another sterilised glass jar until the bubbling subsides, then mix them back together. Add spring water or cool boiled water as needed to keep the chillies submerged. During the second week, the fermentation process will slow down and bubbles will stop forming.

5 Now, remove the seeds: pour the chillies and brine into a large bowl and put on some gloves. Stir the chillies around so that the seeds fall to the bottom of the bowl. Leave them behind but add the chillies to a food processor. When all the chillies have been deseeded, pour the brine through a sieve to remove the remaining seeds. Add the brine to the food processor along with the sherry vinegar.

6 Purée the chillies, brine and vinegar to a fine pulp. Put the mash into a sealed container and keep in the fridge for up to 3 months. Don't be alarmed if the mash fizzes a little.

7 You are now ready to create an infinite amount of your own hot sauce recipes by adding vinegar, tequila, cumin, salt, lime, garlic, coriander or anything else you want to try out. Additionally, once you have a pepper mash, you can use this as a starter for other pepper mashes, much like a sourdough starter (see page 146).

CHIPOTLES

Chipotle peppers feature regularly in our BBQ sauces, stews and the occasional dessert, mainly due to their smoky flavour, but also for their relatively spicy kick. A chipotle pepper is a smoked, dehydrated jalapeño pepper.

To make your own chipotles, start with thoroughly washed fresh red jalapeños. Remove the stems and place them on the rack in a single layer in your smoker or on your grill. As always, make sure to soak your wood chips in water for at least 1 hour beforehand to prevent them burning in the smoker. Fruit-tree woods such as apple or cherry match well with chipotles, but you could use hardwoods, such as oak or beech, if using more easily sourced wood chunks. After a few hours (as much as 12 hours for thicker, fleshier jalapeños) at a low 50-60°C (122-140°F), the jalapeños will have turned black and should be fully dehydrated. Now that you have your own chipotle peppers, what do you do with them? The most popular thing to do is to store them in adobo sauce.

CHIPOTLES IN ADOBO

MAKES 500G

20 dehydrated, smoked chipotle chilli peppers (see opposite)

300g Judas Ketchup (see page 173), or use your usual brand

150ml water

1 large white onion, thinly sliced

4 large cloves garlic, crushed

150ml cider vinegar ½ tsp salt

½ tbsp black peppercorns, freshly cracked

1 Thoroughly wash the chipotle chilli peppers, making sure all stems are fully removed, and place them in a bowl. Cover the chillies with boiling water and weigh them down with a small plate to ensure they are fully submerged. Leave them to soak for 20 minutes.

2 Set aside 6 soaked chipotles. Add the remaining chillies, along with the soaking liquid, to a food processor. Then add the ketchup and measured water. Purée until fully blended.

3 Add the blended chipotle mixture and the reserved whole chipotles to a pan set over a medium heat. Add the onion, garlic, cider vinegar, salt and peppercorns and stir well. Bring to the boil, reduce the heat and allow the chipotles to simmer for about 1¾ hours. Check them after 1 hour: if the sauce has reduced too much, add extra water as needed.

4 Place half the chipotles and adobo in a sterilised jar, seal and store in the fridge. Place the other half in sterilised ice cube trays so you can simply use what you need each time. The jar in the fridge will keep for up to 1 month and the frozen cubes will keep for 3 months.

≡ PICKLES ≡

Pickles are a major accompaniment to US barbecue and it's a match made in heaven. The vinegar cuts through the fat of the meat, enhances its flavour and refreshes your palate for more! You can pickle carrots, onions, cauliflower, beetroot, asparagus and even eggs, but we prefer the crunch of cucumbers, the spice of jalapeños, red onion, mustard seeds and cabbage.

HALF-SOURS
(PICKLED CUCUMBERS)

The secret to getting really crisp, really deliciously cool pickles is to do it the old-fashioned way: fermentation. This recipe is for 'half-sours', or pickles that are half-fermented and finished with a splash of vinegar. It is important that the brine is made with the same ratio of water to salt.

MAKES 1.5 LITRES

10 firm pickling cucumbers, 10–13cm long

6 large sprigs fresh dill, rinsed

6 cloves garlic, peeled

3 tsp Hot Sauce Pepper Mash (see page 176)

1 medium white onion, thinly sliced

3 grape or cherry leaves, rinsed (optional)

6 outer leaves from a green cabbage

300ml white vinegar, for topping up the jars

Red's pickling spice

1 tbsp yellow mustard seeds, toasted

1 tsp fennel seeds, toasted

1 tbsp partly cracked and toasted coriander seeds

1 tbsp partly cracked black peppercorns

1 tbsp partly cracked allspice berries

1 tbsp dill seeds

10 dried bay leaves, crumbled

Brine

1 litre pure filtered or cool boiled water

80g fine sea salt

3 tbsp caster sugar

3 tbsp pickling spice (as above)

1 Make the pickling spice by mixing all the ingredients together in a bowl. Set it aside. Now make the brine. Add the water, salt, sugar and the pickling spice you just made to a saucepan over a medium heat and bring to a boil. When the sugar and salt are fully dissolved remove the pan from the heat and leave to cool while you prepare the cucumbers.

2 Scrub the cucumbers well and slice off the flower end (it contains enzymes that can cause softening). We slice our cucumbers into quarter spears, but you can leave them whole or slice them into rounds for bread-and-butter style pickles.

3 Take 3 sterilised 500ml jars with 2-part preserving lids and place a grape or cherry leaf at the bottom of each, if using.

4 Divide the cucumber spears between jars. (Each jar should hold 10-14 cucumber spears.) Leave at least 2.5cm at the top to be filled with brine. At the same time, intersperse 2 sprigs of fresh dill, 2 cloves of garlic, one-third of the onion slices and 1 teaspoon of Pepper Mash around the spears in each jar.

5 Ladle the cooled brine over the packed cucumbers, making sure the spices are divided evenly. The pickles need to be submerged during fermentation, so make sure everything is packed in tightly.

6 Cover the pickles with a lid or muslin, and leave them to ferment. Depending on how warm or cool your home is, this process can take anywhere between 2-7 days. When small bubbles begin to form on the surface, your pickles are done. When your pickles are at the desired sourness, pour off 2.5cm of brine at the top of the jar, and replace it with white vinegar (100ml in each jar should do it). Adding the vinegar and storing it in the fridge will slow down fermentation. These pickles can be kept sealed in the jars in the fridge for up to 3 months.

WHOLE PICKLED JALAPEÑOS

The over-pickled versions you buy from the supermarket are soggy and have most probably lost their full flavour. Pickling your own meaty jalapeños will result in a fresh, crunchy and super-tasty product. Fajitas at home will never be the same again! If you can't find fresh jalapeños at your local greengrocer, you can order them online from Yorkshire Chilli Farm or South Devon Chilli Farm. Or grow them yourself if you have a south-facing garden. If all else fails, use other chillies like serenade, cayenne, scotch bonnet or habañero.

MAKES AS MANY AS YOU CAN FIT IN THE JAR!

500g whole jalapeño peppers

600ml white vinegar (5 per cent acidity)

125ml water

200g carrots, sliced

100g caster sugar

1 tbsp fine sea salt

1 tbsp Red's Pickling Spice (see page 181)

2 cloves garlic, peeled

1 tsp Hot Sauce Pepper Mash (see page 176) or 1 whole fresh red chilli (optional)

1 Wash the peppers. Leave the stems intact but prick the outer membrane with a sterilised knife tip in 3 or 4 places. Pack them tightly into a sterilised 2-litre pickling jar with a two-part canning lid and set aside.

2 Place the vinegar, water and carrots in a saucepan over a medium heat and bring to the boil. Simmer for 5 minutes, then add the sugar, salt, pickling spice, garlic and pepper mash or chilli (if using) to the saucepan and simmer for a further 5 minutes, stirring to dissolve the ingredients.

3 Pour the liquid over the jalapeños in the jar. Seal and give it a good shake. Be careful not to burn yourself. Leave to cool undisturbed for around 12 hours in a cool, dark place, then label and refrigerate. The peppers will be ready to eat in 1 week and can be stored in the fridge for up to 1 month.

RED ONION PICKLE

You don't find BBQ in Texas without onion and pickle, so we decided to bring the two together and pickle our onions. You can also add ingredients like orange peel, chillies or rosemary.

MAKES 600G

500g red onions, sliced into 7mm rings

½ tsp salt

½ tsp sugar

250ml cider vinegar

1 clove garlic, cut in half

5 black peppercorns, cracked

pared peel from ¼ orange

5 sprigs fresh thyme, leaves picked and stems discarded

1 Fill a kettle with water and turn it on to boil. Meanwhile, put the onion rings into a sieve over the sink. When the kettle has boiled, carefully pour the boiling water over the onion rings to blanch them.

2 Put the salt, sugar, vinegar, garlic, pepper and orange peel into a sterilised 1-litre glass jar. Stir to dissolve the sugar.

3 Add the onions to the jar, as well as the thyme leaves, and stir again to distribute the flavours. Leave to stand for a couple of hours before using. The onions will keep for a few weeks, sealed in a jar in the fridge, but are best used within 1 week.

MUSTARD CAVIAR

This is an adaptation of an Asian-inspired popping condiment. It has an amazing, unique textural quality and goes perfectly with corned beef.

MAKES 700G

250g yellow and brown mustard seeds

200ml cider vinegar

175ml water

175ml white wine

140g caster sugar

1 tbsp flaked sea salt

1 tsp Hot Sauce Pepper Mash (see page 176), or your favourite hot sauce

1 Combine all the ingredients together in a small saucepan and bring to a gentle simmer over a low heat.

2 Cook for about 1 hour, or until the seeds are plump and tender. Top up with water as the liquid evaporates, so the seeds are always submerged.

3 Cool, pour into a sterilised jar and seal. This will keep in the fridge for up to 1 month.

SAUERKRAUT

Sauerkraut is a perfect accompaniment to smoked foods, especially a Reuben Sandwich (see page 58). Done properly, this recipe takes time, however, if you can't wait long enough, we've got another method for achieving similar results more quickly (see Cheat's Sauerkraut, below).

MAKES 1-2KG

1 large white cabbage, around 1–2kg

1 tbsp fine sea salt

1 tsp yellow mustard seeds

1 tsp caraway seeds

1 bay leaf, dried or fresh

1 Peel the outer leaves from the cabbage, then cut into quarters. Remove the core from each wedge and shred the cabbage as thinly as possible. Toss the cabbage in a bowl with the salt, mustard seeds, caraway seeds and bay leaf, distributing all the ingredients evenly.

2 Squeeze the cabbage to break down the leaves for 3 minutes or so. It will start to wilt and will begin to release its juices. At this stage, start packing it into the fermentation crock or glass jar as tightly as possible, avoiding air pockets.

3 Once all the cabbage is in the crock or jar and covered by the juices, cover it loosely with a clean cloth and leave in a cool, dark place, undisturbed for about 1 month, or until it's fermented to your liking. The longer you leave it the softer the cabbage will become.

4 When the sauerkraut is ready, pack it into an airtight sterilised glass jar. It will keep for up to 6 months stored this way.

CHEAT'S SAUERKRAUT

SERVES 6

1 tbsp olive oil

200g speck or smoked bacon, chopped

½ head white cabbage, shredded

½ tsp salt

freshly ground black pepper

60ml pale ale or white wine

60ml cider vinegar

1 tsp caraway seeds

1 tsp yellow mustard seeds

1 dried bay leaf

1 tbsp soft light brown sugar

1 Heat the olive oil in a large saucepan over a high heat. Add the speck or bacon and fry until crisp and golden in colour. Add the shredded cabbage and salt, then grind in some black pepper to taste. Cook, stirring continuously, for 10 minutes, or until the cabbage starts to wilt. Then add the pale ale or white wine, cider vinegar, caraway seeds, mustard seeds, bay leaf and the sugar. Stir everything well to distribute the ingredients.

2 Now turn the heat down low, cover the pan with a lid and continue to cook for a further 20 minutes, or until all the liquid evaporates or has been absorbed into the cabbage. Remove from the heat and leave to cool, ready to be served. Or, you can serve it hot with some home-made Texas Hotlinks (see page 91).

CHAPTER

SNACKS

STUFFED JALAPEÑO POPPERS

Blessed are these righteous morsels, for Red's doth reward our humble mouths with spicy peppers, bubbling cheese and smoky, salty bacon. These are so perfect, you should seriously consider making four or five times the quantity you think you'll need.

SERVES 3-4

75g cream cheese, at room temperature

3 cloves garlic, finely chopped

80g sun-dried tomatoes, finely chopped

1 tbsp Worcestershire sauce

1 tbsp chopped fresh basil leaves

15 large jalapeño peppers (larger peppers are easier to stuff)

15 rashers smoked streaky bacon

flaked sea salt and freshly ground black pepper, to taste

1 In a bowl, combine the cream cheese, garlic, sun-dried tomatoes, Worcestershire sauce and basil. Season with salt and pepper, but remember the grilled bacon will add saltiness.

2 Prepare your grill for medium direct grilling. Meanwhile, slice an opening down one side of each pepper, making sure you don't slice it in half. If you or your guests can't handle the heat, scoop out the seeds from the inside of the peppers, being careful not to break the peppers apart.

3 Using a small spoon, fill each jalapeño pepper with the cream cheese mix, then wrap a rasher of bacon around it so the whole pepper is covered. Secure the bacon with wooden cocktail sticks.

4 Oil the grill grate, place it on the grill, and then arrange the wrapped peppers directly on top. Cook for about 5 minutes, turning occasionally, or until the bacon is crisp and the cheese filling starts to melt. Serve immediately.

BEER-BATTERED PICKLES
DEEP-FRIED

A revolution in deep-fried offerings, the humble pickle has been elevated and is now served like this in many establishments. These little beauties are the perfect accompaniment to an ice-cold beer, while your guests wait patiently for the main event.

SERVES 6

100g plain flour

50g cornflour

1 tsp baking powder

350ml carbonated beer or ale, chilled

sunflower oil, for deep-fat frying

6–10 large dill-pickled gherkins, sliced lengthways about 3mm thick

salt and freshly ground black pepper, to taste

1 Sift 50g of the plain flour with the cornflour and baking powder into a mixing bowl and stir well. Slowly pour the beer into the bowl, whisking constantly to make a batter. A light, crisp coating is best, so the batter needs to be just thick enough to coat the sliced dill pickles. If you prefer a thicker batter, do not use all of the beer. Season with salt and pepper and set aside. Fill your deep-fat fryer with clean oil to the maximum fill level and heat to 175°C (350°F).

2 Meanwhile, place the sliced pickles on a tray or plate lined with kitchen paper to help absorb the pickling vinegar, and leave you with a reasonably dry sliced pickle to deep-fry. Put the remaining flour into another bowl. Add the pickle slices 2 or 3 at a time and toss to coat in the flour.

3 Dunk 2-3 dusted pickle slices into the batter, making sure they get a good coating. Gently lift each pickle out of the batter, and allow the excess batter to run off. Slowly and carefully drop each pickle slice into the deep-fat fryer and fry for 20 seconds on each side (we like to remove the fryer basket from the fryer and use a slotted spoon to turn the pickles to get an even golden colour). Gently keep turning the fried pickles every 10 seconds or so for 1 minute or until the batter is crisp and golden brown in colour.

4 Line another plate or tray with kitchen paper. Once the pickle slices have turned golden brown, lift them out of the oil using a slotted spoon and place them on the kitchen paper to drain. Keep them in a warm place until all the pickles have been coated in batter and deep-fried. Season with salt and pepper, or try some crusts (see Chapter 1) or one of your favourite rubs to add some character. Serve immediately, preferably with cold, frosted glasses of beer.

CRACKLINGS

Your pork butt is in the smoker (see Pulled Pork, page 36) and it's going to take a while to cook. You've already removed the fat cap, and should have a pretty decent piece of perfectly good pigskin. Here's what you do with it while you wait for that butt to smoke.

MAKES 8 SNACKING PORTIONS

pork shoulder fat cap, with skin on

1 tbsp fine sea salt

sunflower oil, for deep-fat frying

salt and freshly ground black pepper, to taste

choice of rub or crust to season (see Chapter 1)

1 Use a sharp knife to remove any excess fat from under the pigskin until you have an equal amount of fat to skin. With the sharp point of the knife, apply just enough pressure to scratch the surface and gently score the skin. Do not cut through it.

2 Sprinkle the salt over the skin. Rub in well, getting it into all the score marks. Cover the skin loosely with cling film and leave it in the fridge for 1 hour to allow the salt to draw out any moisture. Set the smoker to indirect cooking at 120°C (250°F).

3 Remove the skin from the fridge and use kitchen paper to blot off any moisture and to help remove the salt. Put the pigskin into the smoker, skin-side down on the grill, and leave to smoke for 1½ hours. Do not forget to check the wood on the coals. If you need more, add some now.

4 When it is done, take the smoked pigskin from the smoker. It should now feel leathery, but not hard and dry.

5 Set the pigskin aside to cool in the fridge. It will need to be in there for about 1 hour, or until the remaining fats solidify so that it can be cut. When it is ready, take a very sharp knife and cut the skin into 2 x 2cm pieces. Now preheat the deep-fat fryer to 175°C (347°F) and line a baking sheet with kitchen paper.

6 Add all the pieces of skin to the hot oil and deep-fry for 5-10 minutes. Use a slotted spoon to turn and move the cracklings to allow them to cook evenly. When you are happy with the colour and texture, which should be golden brown, crispy and bubbled up, put the skins on the lined baking sheet to drain. Leave the skins to cool before seasoning with salt, pepper and rub or crust.

7 These cracklings can be kept for a day or two at most, wrapped in greaseproof paper. If you are going to refrigerate them, keep in an airtight container. Leave them to come to room temperature again before serving.

CHICKEN SKIN CRACKLINGS

Deep-fried pork cracklings are hugely popular in the BBQ regions of the States. But what if you can't get hold of pigskin? Well, necessity is the mother of invention and in meat-eating South American countries, like Colombia, they've come up with a winner - chicken skin cracklings.

Either choose to make a chicken dish that doesn't need the skins and save the skins for this recipe, or ask your local butcher to put some aside for you. Thigh skins are the best to work with, as they are easy to remove and are generally square in shape. These simple snacks go well alongside the Brunswick Stew (see page 62), and shellfish like the BBQ King Scallops (see page 112).

MAKES 4 DECENT GARNISHES

chicken thigh skins, washed and thoroughly dried

salt, a crust (Chapter 1), for added flavour, or Old Bay-Style Rub (see page 20)

dried chilli flakes (optional)

fresh lime wedges

1 Preheat the oven to 150°C/Gas 2. Lay out the chicken skins evenly on a wire rack set on a baking sheet. Season the skins well with salt or dust them with poultry rub. Place the baking sheet on the middle shelf of the oven and roast for 30-40 minutes, or until the skins are all crispy and golden in colour. Flip them over halfway through cooking, as the edges of the skin will begin to curl up and fat will pool in the middle of the skins. Line another baking sheet with kitchen paper.

2 Remove the skins from the oven, and put them on the prepared baking sheet to drain. Once they are cool enough to handle, gently break them up with your fingers into smaller bite-size pieces and then put them into a serving bowl. Add a few pinches of dried chilli flakes, if using, and serve with lime wedges for squeezing.

CHAPTER

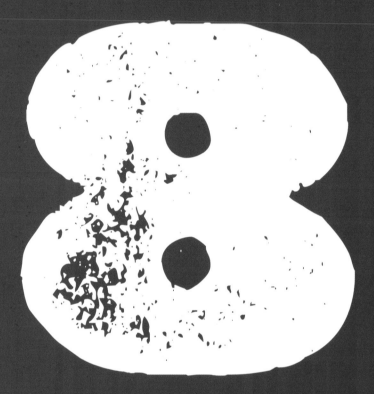

SWEET
STUFF

BANANA PUDDING

When you are eating barbecue three to five times a day, all in the name of research, it's very difficult to find room for dessert. That was until we went to The Pit, in Raleigh, North Carolina, where the pitmaster forced an amazing banana pudding on us.

SERVES 6

250ml whole milk

½ tsp salt

4 eggs, separated

½ tsp vanilla extract

397g can condensed milk

1 tbsp plain flour

8 square or rectangular trifle sponges
(we recommend Lyons brand)

4 ripe bananas

Meringue

125g caster sugar

2 tbsp cornflour

1 Place a heavy-based saucepan over a medium heat. Add the milk and bring to a simmer, then add the salt. Remove from the heat. Whisk the egg yolks (transferring the whites to a clean bowl for making the meringue) with the vanilla extract, condensed milk and flour, ensuring you beat lots of air into the mixture. Stir the egg mixture into the saucepan of warm milk and return to the hob. Whisk over a low heat, stirring continuously, until the mixture starts to thicken and, when you lift the whisk out of the mixture, it leaves ribbons behind. This should take 5-10 minutes max. Remove from the heat. Pour the custard into a clean bowl to stop it cooking further.

2 To maximise the sponge, cut each sponge into 3 pieces, by laying it flat on the work surface and pressing down with the palm of your hand and running a knife through it.

3 Peel and slice the bananas into rounds. Take a level portion of custard and pour evenly into a suitable dish, or trifle bowl. Add a layer of sponge, then some banana slices and then another ladleful of custard. Repeat until all the ingredients are used up, making sure you finish with a layer of custard, so the bananas do not blacken. Put the dish in the fridge to cool.

4 Now make the meringue. Using a hand-held electric mixer on medium speed, whisk the egg whites, and as soon as they start to increase in volume, add some caster sugar, a little at a time. This is a slow process, but keep at it until all the sugar is incorporated and no longer grainy. Lastly, beat in the cornflour.

5 When ready to serve, take the cooled banana and custard out of the fridge and spoon over the meringue. Be creative and make peaks, swirls and mounds in the meringue. Brown the top, either under a grill or, if you have one, with a chef's blow torch, but keep a close eye on it to avoid burning the meringue - aim for a golden brown, crisp finish.

PEANUT AND CHOCOLATE BUTTER AND CHEESECAKE

Peanut butter in its modern form was created in North America after all, so Red's had no choice but to create a sweet on the menu that would reflect this obsession. Probably the most popular dessert on the menu, this cheesecake is simple to make, but be warned, it's unbelieveably moreish.

SERVES 12

Base
250g plain digestive biscuits

20g unsweetened cocoa powder

125g unsalted butter, melted

Filling
120g smooth peanut butter

300g caster sugar

1kg mascarpone cheese

50ml double cream

10ml vanilla extract

Topping
200ml double cream

200g milk chocolate, broken into pieces

1 If you have a food processor, use the blade attachment to crush the digestive biscuits. Alternatively, place them in a plastic bag, seal securely and bash the biscuits with a rolling pin. Place the crumbs in a bowl and add the cocoa powder. Stir well and pour in the melted butter.

2 Place a 24cm mousse ring or cake tin with a removable base on a baking sheet. Press the crumbs into the base of the ring or tin using the back of a spoon to distribute evenly, slightly pushing them up the side of the tin. Put the base in the fridge while you make the filling.

3 In a large mixing bowl, cream together the peanut butter and sugar. Carefully fold in the mascarpone cheese, double cream and vanilla extract but do not over-mix as this might cause the mixture to split.

4 Take the set base out of the fridge and spoon the filling on top. Use the back of a spoon or a palette knife to make the surface as level as possible. Put the cheesecake back into the fridge on the baking sheet while you make the chocolate topping.

5 Place a saucepan over a medium heat and add the double cream. Bring it slowly to the boil then remove it from the heat and add the milk chocolate. Mix well until all the chocolate has melted. Leave it to cool for 10 minutes, and then pour it evenly over the chilled cheesecake. Lift the baking sheet and very gently tilt it around so the chocolate spreads evenly over the cheesecake. Return the cheesecake to the fridge to set.

6 When you are ready to serve the cheesecake, remove the whole thing from the tin and put it on a board or plate for slicing. Take a sharp knife, dip it in hot water and run it along the inside of the tin to loosen the cheesecake from the ring. To slice the cake, dunk your knife into hot water to warm the blade. Dry the blade with a tea towel, and slice the cheesecake into portions. Repeat for each slice.

TOASTED
MARSHMALLOWS

Marshmallow is surprisingly easy to make at home, and you can add your own little twist to bring some variety to the boring vanilla-flavoured ones available in your supermarket. This recipe uses fresh raspberries, but you can use most soft fruits, such as strawberries, blueberries or blackberries.

SERVES 6

vegetable oil, for brushing

125ml water

3 sheets of leaf gelatine

340g caster sugar

225g light golden syrup

¼ tsp salt

2 tsp vanilla extract

120g icing sugar

120g cornflour

8 fresh raspberries

1 Brush a 30 x 20cm baking tray with vegetable oil and set aside. Put 60ml of the water in the bowl of a stand mixer fitted with the whisk attachment and add the gelatine sheets. Stir briefly with a wooden spoon to make sure all of the gelatine is in contact with water and leave it to soften while you make the syrup.

2 Heat the sugar, golden syrup, salt and remaining water in a small heavy-based saucepan over a low heat, stirring until sugar has dissolved. Then raise the heat to medium and, without stirring, bring the mixture to the boil. Continue to heat the mixture until a sugar thermometer registers 115°C. Remove from the heat and let stand until any bubbles dispel.

3 Turn the mixer on to a low speed and slowly pour the hot syrup into the gelatine and water mixture, drizzling it in a thin stream down the side of the bowl. When all of the syrup has been added, increase the speed to high and beat for about 5 minutes until the mixture is very thick. Whisk in the vanilla extract until fully combined. If you don't have access to a stand mixer, use a whisk, following the same process.

4 Mix the icing sugar and cornflour together. Dust the oiled tray with half the icing sugar and cornflour mixture, spoon in half the marshmallow mixture and scatter the raspberries over the top. Cover with the remaining mixture, smoothing the top. Leave to stand, uncovered, at room temperature for 2-3 hours, or until the surface is not sticky and you can gently pull the marshmallow away from the sides of the tray.

5 Dust a chopping board with icing sugar. Use a spatula to pull the sides of marshmallow from the edge of tray, then invert on to the chopping board. Dust the top with icing sugar and cornflour. Cut the marshmallow into cubes and coat in more icing sugar, shaking off the excess.

6 To serve, place a marshmallow on the end of a long metal skewer, then cook on the grill or over a campfire and eat as close to bubbling without singeing your lips. These will keep in the fridge, packed between layers of greaseproof paper, for up to 1 month.

SUGAR RING DONUTS

Anyone who has been to Red's will know our famous Donut Burger - the holy union of sweet and meat (see page 76). If you're feeling adventurous, here's a simple recipe to make awesome home-made donuts so you can build your very own. We recommend using a thermostat-controlled deep-fat fryer. Please do not use an old-fashioned chip pan, as they are seriously dangerous.

MAKES 10 DONUTS

350ml whole milk

70g lard

2 x 7g packets dried instant yeast

80ml warm water

2 eggs at room temperature, beaten

50g caster sugar

1½ tsp salt

1 tsp freshly grated nutmeg

650g plain flour, plus extra for dusting

vegetable oil, for deep-frying

Glaze

60ml whole milk

1 tsp vanilla extract

250g icing sugar

1 Place the milk in a saucepan over a medium heat and warm until hot enough to melt the lard - test by adding a little piece. Add the lard and set the saucepan aside while it melts. Meanwhile, in a separate bowl, mix the yeast with the warm water and leave it to dissolve for 5 minutes.

2 When the lard has melted and the yeast has dissolved, place both in the bowl of a stand mixer with a paddle attachment. Add the eggs, sugar, salt, nutmeg and half the flour and mix on low speed at first, then increase the speed until the flour is incorporated. Turn the speed up to medium and beat until well combined. Add the remaining flour, mix on low speed at first, and then increase the speed to medium to beat well.

3 Change the mixer attachment to a dough hook and beat on medium speed until the dough pulls away from the inside of the bowl and becomes smooth. Transfer to a well-oiled bowl, cover loosely and leave to rise for 1 hour, or until doubled in size.

4 On a well floured surface, roll out the dough to 1cm thick. Cut out using a 6.5cm pastry ring, then using a 2cm ring, cut another hole in the centre. Put the rings on a floured baking sheet, cover lightly with a clean tea towel and leave to rise for 30 minutes, or until doubled in size.

5 Preheat the oil in a deep-fat fryer. When it reaches 185°C, gently place 3 or 4 donuts into the oil using a slotted spoon. Cook for 1 minute on each side, then lift them out one at a time and place them on a wire rack. Cook the remaining dough rings in the same way, then leave to cool for 15-20 minutes.

6 Meanwhile, make the glaze by placing a saucepan over a low heat. Add the milk and vanilla and heat until warm. Sift the icing sugar into the milk mixture and whisk slowly until well combined. Remove the glaze from the heat and set over a bowl of warm water. Dip the donuts into the glaze, one at a time, and let them drain on a wire rack placed on a baking sheet for 5 minutes before serving.

TOASTED MARSHMALLOW SWEET POTATO PIE

Sweet potatoes are a Thanksgiving classic. Mash 'em with some sugar, pecans and marshmallows and it's unclear as to whether you have a side or dessert.

SERVERS 12

500g sweet potatoes

250ml buttermilk

3 eggs, lightly beaten

175g soft light brown sugar

¼ tsp salt

300g large marshmallows (2.5cm size),
home-made (see page 204)
or shop-bought

150g mini marshmallows (85mm size),
home-made or shop-bought

Pastry

100g icing sugar

125g unsalted butter

1 egg, plus 1 egg yolk

250g plain flour, plus extra
for dusting

1 Make the pastry by mixing the icing sugar and butter together in a food processor, using the blade attachment. Add the whole egg, process briefly, then add the egg yolk and process again. Next, add all the flour and mix until a smooth dough forms. Remove the dough from the food processor, wrap it in cling film, then put it in the fridge to rest for 1 hour.

2 Preheat the oven to 160°C/Gas 3. Remove the pastry from the fridge, unwrap it and roll it out on a floured surface to the thickness of a £1 coin. Transfer the pastry to a greased 22cm tart tin, using your fingers to press the dough firmly into all the nooks and crannies but leaving some of the dough hanging over the edges. Use a fork to prick holes into the base of the pastry case. Line the pastry with baking parchment, and fill the case with pie weights or baking beans. Blind bake for 10-15 minutes, then take the pastry out of the oven and remove the baking parchment and weights. Bake the pastry for a further 5 minutes, or until the pastry is lightly browned. Remove from the oven and leave to cool completely.

3 Meanwhile, pierce the sweet potatoes and boil them in a large pan of water for 20-30 minutes, or until soft. Let them cool, then peel. Using a food processor, pulse the sweet potato flesh until smooth. Add the buttermilk and process briefly, then add the eggs, brown sugar and salt. Pulse for another 30 seconds. Increase the oven temperature to 180°C/Gas 4.

4 Pour the filling into the prepared pastry case. Tidy up the pastry edges with a sharp knife. Bake the pie for about 50 minutes, or until the centre is just set and puffed and the pastry is golden. Remove the pie from the oven, turn off the oven and preheat the grill to medium.

5 Cover the top of the pie with the large marshmallows, piling them up in the middle. Fill any empty spaces with the mini marshmallows. Place the pie on a baking sheet and set under the grill for just under a minute, or until browned. Be very careful not to burn the topping.

6 Turn off the grill and leave the pie in the oven for about 3 minutes, or until the marshmallow topping just softens. Remove from the oven and place on a wire rack to cool slightly before serving.

CLASSIC WAFFLES

Waffles are a popular Belgian speciality, often served by street vendors, with all kinds of toppings available. But this treat has found its way to the dinner table in the southern states of America, where it is well and truly regarded as 'soul food', served with fried chicken and lashings of maple syrup or white gravy. You would be forgiven if you thought this to be a truly disgusting marriage, but never say never, because it works!

We serve waffles with fried bananas, whipped cream and berries, or smoked streaky bacon, fried eggs and maple syrup to kick-start the day and blow away the cobwebs of the night before. You can buy waffle irons for under £30 online; electric waffle makers are more expensive, but a great investment nonetheless.

MAKES 8

260g plain flour

1 tsp salt

20g baking powder

50g caster sugar

non-stick baking spray

2 eggs

370ml warm whole milk

75g unsalted butter, melted

1 tsp vanilla extract

1 In a large bowl, mix together the flour, salt, baking powder and sugar. Spray the waffle iron with non-stick baking spray and preheat it to a medium-high temperature. If you are using a hot-coal waffle iron, stick it in the fire now to heat up. The hotter you get your waffle iron, the darker and crispier the finished waffles will be.

2 Place the eggs in a separate bowl and beat them. Stir in the milk, butter and vanilla extract, then pour into the flour mixture. Whisk until just blended.

3 Ladle the batter into the preheated prepared waffle iron and cook the waffles for around 5 minutes or until golden and crisp. Serve immediately with toppings of your choice.

MRS MUNRO'S AWARD-WINNING CARAMEL *PECAN PIE*

Wives know best: always have, always will. This was proved correct at the 2011 Mayhem in May BBQ competition where the struggling boys, all focused on the meat category, were embarrassingly pipped to first prize by a dessert pulled together by Mrs Munro. And while every husband will put his wife on a pedestal, Red's really does have Mrs Munro to thank for this comforting recipe and trophy gold. Best served hot with cream or ice cream.

SERVES 12

Pastry

100g icing sugar

125g unsalted butter

1 egg, plus 1 egg yolk

250g plain flour, plus extra
for dusting

Filling

2 x 410g cans Carnation caramel

6 Granny Smith apples

1 tbsp ground cinnamon

1½ tsp fresh lemon juice

1½ tsp vanilla extract

1 tbsp cornflour

45g caster sugar

splash of milk

Crumble topping

50g unsalted butter, softened

100g soft light brown sugar

200g plain flour

150g pecans, broken up

1 Make the pastry by creaming together the icing sugar and butter in a food processor, using the blade attachment. Add the whole egg and pulse to blend, followed by the egg yolk. Next, add all the flour and mix to a smooth dough. Remove the dough from the food processor, wrap it in cling film and put it in the fridge for 1 hour.

2 Preheat the oven to 160°C/Gas 3. Take the pastry out of the fridge, unwrap it and roll it out on a floured surface to the thickness of a £1 coin. Transfer the pastry into a 23cm greased tart case or pie tin and use your fingers to press the dough firmly into all the nooks and crannies but leaving some of the dough hanging over the edges. Prick holes into the base of the tart case with a fork. Line the pastry with baking parchment, and fill the tart case with pie weights or baking beans. Bake blind for 10-15 minutes, then take the pastry out of the oven and remove the baking parchment and weights. Bake the pastry for a further 5 minutes, or until the pastry is lightly browned. Remove from the oven and leave to cool.

3 Once cooled, remove any excess pastry from the edges with a sharp knife, and add the filling. Spoon most of the caramel into the pastry case, but reserve 1 tablespoon to pour over the pie before baking. Peel and core the apples, then slice each into paper-thin slivers, sprinkle on the caster sugar, vanilla extract and lemon juice, and gently mix them with the cinnamon and cornflour. Arrange the slices on top of the caramel and set aside.

4 Make the crumble topping by placing the butter, soft light brown sugar and flour into a large mixing bowl. You could use a food processor to make the crumble topping, but it's better to use your hands for this stage so you get a more rustic crumble, with some larger chunks to chew on.

5 Add the chopped pecan and mix well. Pour the pecan crumble over the top of the filling evenly, making sure the apple slices are covered. Put a little splash of milk into the caramel tins to dilute the remaining caramel, then drizzle this over the top of the pie. Place the pie on the middle shelf of the oven, and bake for 30 minutes at 160°C, or until the crumble is golden.

PECAN AND SALTED CARAMEL PEACH COBBLER

A traditional cobbler topping is usually made with a batter, but after a visit to one of our favourite smokehouses in Dallas, Texas, where they use a biscuit-based topping instead, we decided to come up with our own take on this American dessert.

SERVES 8

Dough topping

100g unsalted butter, softened

125g icing sugar

1 tsp vanilla extract

125g pecans, roughly chopped

150g plain flour

Filling

6 large peaches, firm to the touch and not over-ripe

100g unsalted butter

150g soft light brown sugar

1 vanilla pod or 1 tsp vanilla extract

300ml double cream

½ tsp sea salt

1 First make the topping. Beat the softened butter with the icing sugar in a bowl until light and creamy. Add the vanilla, pecans and flour, then knead everything together into a dough. Wrap the dough in cling film and put it into the fridge until needed.

2 Now for the filling. Preheat the oven to 180°C/Gas 4. Cut the peaches in half and remove the stones. Place a saucepan over a medium heat, add the butter and sugar (reserving 1 tablespoon for later) and allow them to melt gently. Split the vanilla pod in half and add it to the pan, or add the extract, if using.

3 Add the peaches to the mixture in the pan and slowly cook them on both sides for about 10 minutes, using tongs to turn and coat them in the sauce until they start to caramelise and the sauce begins to turn golden brown. Remove the peaches and place them in an ovenproof dish.

4 Slowly add the cream to the sauce and turn up the heat. Stir well until all the cream is incorporated and then simmer gently, stirring until toffee in colour and thickened. Add the salt. Remove the vanilla pod, if using, and pour half the toffee sauce over the peaches. Remove the pecan dough from the fridge, unwrap and crumble it into small pebble-sized pieces over the peaches. Finally, sprinkle over the reserved tablespoon of light brown sugar, which will caramelise during the bake to add depth and texture to the crumble.

5 Place the dish on the middle shelf of the oven and bake for 15-20 minutes or until golden brown.

6 Pour the remainder of the toffee sauce, which should still be warm, over the cobbler and serve with clotted cream or vanilla ice cream.

SWEETIE POPS

Kids love ice lollies, but they really love these little beauties which are bejewelled with suspended jelly sweets. You can reduce the amount of sugar if you prefer, but the recipe below already takes the kids-go-crazy-on-sugar factor into consideration.

MAKES 12

200g caster sugar

500ml water

1 litre unsweetened apple juice

250ml unsweetened pineapple or orange juice

125ml fresh lemon juice

1 bag of jellied sweets such as Haribo Starmix or Tangfastics

12 ice lolly moulds or 12 paper cups and wooden lolly sticks

1 Put the sugar into a large saucepan, add the water and bring to the boil. Reduce the heat and simmer, uncovered, for 3-4 minutes or until the sugar is dissolved, stirring occasionally.

2 Remove the pan from the heat and stir in the fruit juices. While the liquid is still warm, add the sweets and stir them through just to melting point. You want to melt the sugar on the outside of the sweets, but still keep the shape of the sweet. Allow the mixture to cool.

3 Prepare the ice lolly moulds. Half fill the moulds or cups with the juice mixture, then divide half of the sweets between them with a spoon. Do not top the moulds with the holders at this point. Freeze until firm.

4 Remove the frozen lollies from the freezer and top each one up with the remaining liquid and again divide the rest of the sweets between them. Top the moulds with the holders and freeze again until frozen.

CHAPTER

DRINKS

ICED TEA & RED'S ICED TEA

Stop off at any good 'cue joint in the US, and you'll find vats of free iced tea to cool the soul and quench the thirst brought on by the salty rub of the meat. In the restaurant we offer it up straight, and with an edge (bourbon, dark rum and orange Curaçao). This switch-up is like a bolt from the old man upstairs and is well worth a try on a hot, lazy summer afternoon.

SERVES 1

Iced tea

25ml fresh lemon juice

25ml honey syrup (see tip, below)

50ml cold breakfast tea

Red's iced tea

½ tsp Appleton VX rum

½ tsp Wild Turkey 81 bourbon

½ tsp Orange Curaçao

25ml honey syrup (see tip, below)

25ml fresh lemon juice

25ml cold breakfast tea

ice cubes

lemon slice, to garnish

To make honey syrup, put equal quantities of honey and water in a small saucepan and place over a medium heat. Stir until the honey has melted into the water, then remove from the heat and leave to cool.

1 Pour all the ingredients, except the ice cubes and lemon slices into a cocktail shaker, seal and shake well for about 15 seconds.

2 Add some ice cubes to a glass and strain in your iced tea. Garnish with a thin slice of lemon.

MELONADE

There's much to be said for drinking bourbon and letting the mind wander. When we were in Memphis, Tennessee, sitting outside the RV park at 3AM, Greg, our IT geek, came up with the idea of this refreshing drink. Remarkably, he could still remember it in the morning.

SERVES 8

1 whole galia or honeydew melon, skinned and deseeded

50g caster sugar

1 tsp ground ginger

ice cubes

lemonade, to top up

gin (optional)

1 Cut the melon into 3cm cubes and put them into a heatproof jug or bowl. Sprinkle in the sugar and ginger. Pour in just enough boiling water to reach the top of the diced melon, then set aside to cool.

2 Once the water has cooled, tip everything into a blender and blitz until smooth.

3 Pour this thick melon syrup into a large jug, filled halfway with ice, and top up with lemonade. Mix well and serve. For grown-ups, add a few good measures of gin if you like.

BOURBON *BACON* BLITZ

Everything tastes better with bacon, right? Then add bourbon. Can any two words sound better? Only when you add chocolate. That's right, believers. This shake combines all three. It works, and then some.

SERVES 1

50ml Wild Turkey 81 bourbon

300ml cold whole milk

4 scoops chocolate ice cream

4 ice cubes

1 rasher crispy smoked streaky bacon, torn into shards

1 Put all the ingredients, except the bacon, into a blender and whizz.

2 Pour the mixture into a large glass, then garnish with shards of crispy bacon. Sit back and prepare to be amazed.

JULEP

For centuries the Mint Julep has been a staple cocktail of America's Deep South, best known for its popularity at events such as the Kentucky Derby. The use of mint gives a refreshing edge to the smoky, barrel-aged bourbon flavour. No need for a straw here - slow sipping is the appropriate way to sup.

SERVES 1

fresh mint leaves, plus extra sprigs to garnish

½ tsp sugar syrup
(1:1 sugar and water mix)

50ml bourbon
(such as Wild Turkey 81)

crushed ice

1 Add 4-5 mint leaves and the sugar syrup to the glass and gently bruise the mint with the back of a spoon to release its flavour.

2 Add the bourbon and fill the glass with crushed ice. Mix it up with the spoon, add a final dome of crushed ice and garnish with a generous hedge of mint, stalks and all, to give a punchy aroma.

BLOODY PIG

We've twice-blessed the classic Bloody Mary with a few of Red's staple pantry items to give you two new recipes to add to your black book. Make it as spicy as you wish with all the goodness of sweet tomato and a stern slap from Sweden's best vodka.

This recipe requires a little forward planning, as you need to infuse a bottle of vodka with bacon flavour (also called fat-washing), 24 hours prior to serving. It's dead straightforward, though, and the infusing makes all the difference. You'll need a Boston shaker - a two-piece shaker that has a metal bottom and mixing glass - and a 1-litre airtight container.

SERVES 1

50ml bacon-infused Absolut vodka

75ml tomato juice, chilled

5ml or 1 tsp pickle brine (gherkin)

ice cubes

1 celery stick

Infusion

1 litre Absolut vodka

300g pack of smoked streaky bacon

Spiking ingredients

Tabasco sauce

celery salt

Worcestershire sauce

lemon juice

freshly cracked black pepper

1 First, make the vodka infusion. Slowly fry all but one of the rashers of smoked streaky bacon to release all of the fat. Pour the vodka into a 1-litre airtight container, add the bacon and fat and keep refrigerated for 24 hours. This infusion will keep for about a week in the fridge. Strain through a fine sieve before using.

2 To make the cocktail, add the strained vodka, tomato juice and pickle brine to the cocktail shaker. Add the spiking ingredients to taste and then add cubed ice until the shaker is full.

3 Meanwhile, prepare the bacon rasher for garnishing by gently frying until crispy on both sides. You want to keep the rasher as long as possible so it doesn't get lost in the glass when serving.

4 Gently pour the mixture from the shaker into a glass filled with ice. Don't mix as the ice in the shaker helps to chill the drink but does not dilute or compromise the texture of the tomato juice. Garnish with the celery stick and crispy bacon rasher.

BLOODY MARY - BLOODY COW

This was originally created for hungry dads as an accompaniment to our Father's Day Holy Cow burger which contained 17 types of beef from smoked ox heart to a Wagyu patty. The jerky included in this recipe MUST be of the best quality available, as the drink itself does not require much, but you won't be able to stop nibbling during preparation.

SERVES 1

50ml vodka infusion (as below)

5ml or 1 tsp pickle brine (from a jar of gherkins)

15ml or 1 tbsp Tio Pepe

75ml plain tomato passata (passed through a fine sieve lined with muslin to clarify)

5ml or 1 tsp green Tabasco sauce

1 tsp Worcestershire sauce

ice cubes

½ tsp jerky dust or shavings

½ tsp cayenne pepper

½ tsp celery salt

wedge of lemon

Vodka infusion

1 tbsp wholegrain mustard

1 tbsp cayenne pepper

1 tbsp dried chilli flakes

250ml Absolut vodka

Garnish

twist of lemon peel

fresh basil

15–20cm shard of Beef Jerky
(see page 68)

1 Make the vodka infusion. Mash the mustard, cayenne and chilli flakes into a paste in a pestle and mortar. Pour the vodka into a jar with a lid, add the paste mixture, seal and leave for at least 30 minutes to infuse. Pass the mixture through a fine sieve lined with muslin into a clean jar to clarify.

2 Add all the wet ingredients to the cocktail shaker and top up with cubed ice. Gently blend, taking care not to dilute the drink too much.

3 Mix the jerky dust, cayenne and celery salt and pour the mixture onto a small, flat plate. Rub the wedge of lemon around the rim of a highball glass so it picks up a coating of juice. Upend the glass into the jerky dust mixture so some adheres to the rim of the glass. Pour your cocktail and garnish with the lemon peel twist, fresh basil and jerky shard.

GEORGIA HOBO JUICE

Taking inspiration from the rambling musings of a very drunk man we met outside Atlanta airport isn't the most common starting point for making a new cocktail, but this is Red's, so anything can happen. Despite the lack of real Moonshine, we've tried to replicate the age-old classic among the modern-day moonshiners of America's South.

SERVES 1

50ml corn whisky

25ml fresh lemon juice

25ml fresh lime juice

25ml sugar syrup

lemonade, to top up

lemon and lime slices,
to garnish

1 Add all the ingredients to a cocktail shaker. Seal with the lid and shake. Strain into a glass, add garnish, and if you have a brown paper bag to hand, make use of it for the true moonshiner's touch.

MICHELADA

This Mexican beer cocktail is really popular in our restaurant and it's great with oysters on a hot summer evening after a long day at work. If you like beer and Bloody Marys, this is the perfect drink for you! Best served really cold in big glasses, such as trigger beer mugs that have been in the freezer for a couple of hours.

SERVES 4

1 litre or 3 bottles of light Mexican beer, such as Corona or Pacifico Clara, chilled

1 litre tomato juice, chilled

125ml fresh lime juice

15ml Tabasco or other hot sauce

25ml Worcestershire sauce

1 tsp Basic Dry Rub
(see page 16)

1 tbsp table salt

1 tsp cayenne pepper

5 lime wedges, for rimming
and serving

4 live oysters (optional)

ice cubes

1 Pour the beer, tomato juice and lime juice into a large jug and add the hot sauce, Worcestershire sauce and basic dry rub.

2 Mix the salt and cayenne pepper on a plate. Rub the top of each glass with a lime wedge, then press the rim in the salt and cayenne until coated.

3 Put plenty of ice in the glasses, pour in the Michelada and top with an oyster, if using. Garnish with the remaining lime wedges. If you want your drink a little spicier, add a few more drops of hot sauce to the glass once served.

PICKLEBACK

The pickleback is a strange combination of a shot of whisky, chased by a shot of pickle juice. The chaser helps neutralise the initial burn of the alcohol, then pulls out more of the deep flavours hidden within the whisky, giving a smooth, rich taste sensation, not dissimilar to a liquid Big Mac. Like the Donut Burger, this shouldn't work, but does. Again and again.

SERVES 1

25ml Jameson's Irish Whisky

25ml pickle brine (see page 181)

1 Fill one shot glass with whisky and fill a second one with pickle brine. Shoot the whisky and chase with the pickle juice. Repeat as required.

THE PERFECT HANGOVER CURE: THE HOLY GRAIL

Hangovers are commonplace at Red's - it goes with the territory. So when the chance came up to develop The Holy Grail - a cure - there was only one place to go for the land's greatest apothecaries: our believers.

A call to action on Red's Facebook and Twitter pages summoned a host of doctors, physicians, pharmacologists and biologists, all throwing their (drinking) gloves into the ring to help. A special Red's thanks to Steve Livesey MPharm and Dr Matt Humphries PhD, MSc, BSc for their shared wisdom and knowledge to help develop this drink. The Holy Grail is based on an oral rehydration solution with a twist, plus a few extra magic ingredients. It will go a long way to addressing the core elements of your hangover: dehydration; loss of salts, vitamins and electrolytes, such as potassium and magnesium; and low glucose levels.

SERVES 1

2 large bananas (preferably slightly brown)

250g caramel ice cream
(use vanilla as alternative)

330ml coconut water

3–4 tsp Horlicks
small handful of almonds

large handful of fresh berries
(blueberries or raspberries)

semi-skimmed milk, to top up the blender (about 200ml)

pinch salt, to taste

1 Place all the ingredients, except the salt, into the blender and blitz.

2 When everything is mixed and the nuts have broken up into drinkable-sized pieces, add a small pinch of salt and continue to whizz for 30 seconds. Taste and, if necessary, add a little more salt, being careful not to add too much or you'll ruin the taste. Then simply pour the mixture into your glass and let it bless your soul.

MAKE YOUR OWN...
BEER
with our pal Luke Raven

Brewing beer works on exactly the same principal as cooking; combining ingredients in a particular way to create an awesome taste. It's about timing, quality ingredients and - above all - passion and love. The better the ingredients and the more passion you put into your creation, the more enjoyment you'll get from drinking and sharing it!

Scott, James and I spent hours drinking beers and eating meat to decide what we should brew, and we all agreed that the noble India Pale Ale (IPA) was the main contender worthy to complement the big-hitting flavours of low and slow barbecue.

IPAs were created to slake the thirst for beer in the British colonies in India. Back then, British beer was traditionally quite weak, in both flavour and strength. To survive the long journey, beers were brewed to a higher strength and more hops than usual were added; thus a new stronger breed of beer was born. As new trade routes opened, so more hops were cultivated in warmer climes and the beer industry grew. Not long ago every household used to make their own beer. The 'Public House' was simply the house on the street where the best beer was made. So go forth with this Red's IPA, experiment, brew, imbibe and welcome the masses to your own public house. Amen.

MAKING THE RED'S IPA

You can make beer in exactly the same way you would in a brewery, using real grain and hops, without spending bucks. Check out your local homebrew store, or even contact a local brewery and ask if they'll let you have a small amount of ingredients. See page 246 for information on homebrew equipment.

MAKES 60 PINTS

Malted Barley

4.3kg pale malt

500g wheat malt

200g crystal

Hops

Bittering hop:
22g Galena

Late addition hops:
25g Amarillo

25g Citra

THE GRAIN

We want four things from the grain: starches, enzymes, colour and flavour. You'll generally get the grain pre-milled, although if it's not, you can mill it (crack it) yourself by constructing a mill: set two rollers about 10mm apart, et voila! Beer, by definition, must contain at least 50 per cent malted barley, although you can of course add other types of grain (oats, rye, wheat, etc). The majority of beers use a pale malt for the bulk of the recipe. You would usually use 4-7kg of base malt per 20 litres, depending on the style of beer. For our IPA, we opt for a combination of pale malt, wheat malt and a little crystal malt to add body, colour and depth. Crystal malts have been partially roasted, and some of the non-fermentable sugars have started to caramelise, so these will typically add sweetness as well as a little golden colour.

1 MASHING

We need to convert the starch into sugar (which the yeast will then use to ferment on and create alcohol). Add hot water (76°C) to the grains to awaken the enzymes - you're creating what's called the 'wort'. Add 1 litre of water for every 500g of grain. It's very important to add the water and grain together, as gently and uniformly as possible. You don't want any dry clumps, puddles or hot spots. The overall temperature should be 64-70°C. The beta amylase enzymes are active toward the 63°C end, which make fermentable sugars, making a dry beer. The alpha amylase enzymes are active toward the 71°C end, making unfermentable sugars, resulting in a sweet beer. The balance is up to you, in this case, we're looking for an optimum temperature of around 68°C. Insulate the mash tun by wrapping it up in a blanket for 1 hour. While you're mashing, start heating 2 litres of water per 500g grain, so in this case 20 litres. You're aiming for 80-90°C.

2 TESTING THE WORT

After about 1 hour, the conversion from starch to sugar should be complete. To test this, put a small amount of wort on a white surface (like a plate) and add a drop of iodine. If it turns black, starches still exist and it needs to sit longer.

3 SPARGING

This is the process of rinsing the hot wort from the grain. Take the first couple of litres from the bottom of the mash tun and pour back onto the grain bed to filter out husks, as these can cause off-flavours when boiled. Next, fully drain the wort, add half the sparge water (10 litres) and let it sit for 20 minutes. Drain. Then do it again. Continue sparging until your pre-boil volume is reached: you're aiming for about 23 litres for a 1 hour boil - this will leave you with a 20-litre batch of lovely beer.

4 BOILING

Bring the temperature up to 100°C. Stir the wort occasionally whilst it is getting up to temperature. While the beer is coming up to boil, you can prepare your hops and your fermenters.

Hops

Hops add aroma, flavour and bitterness to the beer, providing a balance against the sweetness of the sugars. Where they're grown determines the flavour. The fuller flavour ones are often grown in more temperate regions, whilst British hops are extremely versatile for bittering and aroma. American hops are very popular for bold flavours and aromas. For the Red's IPA we selected three American hops; Galena for mellow bittering, and Citra and Amarillo for distinctive citrus and fruit characteristics. Hops also contain essential oils called alpha acids. The higher the alpha acid percentage and time boiled, the more bitter it will be. Four to five per cent is about average and 10-12 per cent is high. For aroma, add higher alpha acid hops just at the end of the wort boil, as you turn the heat off.

Fermenters

Brewing is 90 per cent cleaning and sanitising - yeast will feed on absolutely anything, including cleaning chemicals, so it won't take much to spoil your beer. However, DO NOT scrub plastic fermenters! Microscopic scratches in plastic harbour wild yeast and bacteria that will destroy your beer. It's better to let the sterilising solution sit for 20 minutes, then rinse with clean filtered water twice.

5 ADDING THE HOPS

Boil the wort for 1 hour at a rolling boil. The more vigorous a boil the better. Once the wort is boiling add the bittering hops, Galena. 22g of full leaf for this IPA (pellets equate to 90 per cent of the weight of full leaf hops). Fifteen minutes before the end of the hour add the first addition of flavouring hops: 5g each of Amarillo and Citra. Ten minutes before the end of the boil add a further 10g each of those same hops. Finally, 5 minutes from the end, add another 10g each of the aroma hops. What we're doing here is building up extra layers of flavour and aroma, and giving the beer balance. Then, simply turn off the heat.

6 CHILLING THE WORT

It's really important to chill the boiled wort down from 100°C to 21°C (your target: the optimum temperature for yeast) as fast as possible. Beer is the most susceptible to infection at around 60°C.

7 FILL THE FERMENTER

Pour the finished wort into the fermentation bucket, making sure to remove the hops by sieving. Seal and shake it to add a little oxygen (needed to kickstart the aerobic yeast reproduction). Whilst the wort is 20-23°C 'pitch' (add) the yeast.

8 YEAST

If using dry yeast, rehydrate with a small amount of warm water before pitching.

9 TRANSFER

After 1-2 weeks of primary fermentation, transfer to a clean and sanitised secondary container/fermenter to clear the beer up and let it condition. Use a sanitised siphon to get the beer from the primary to the secondary. The beer will have most of the alcohol in it already so it will be more resistant to nasties in the air.

10 BOTTLE

Soak the bottles in a sanitiser for at least 5 minutes. Do not rinse. Place bottles on a sanitised dishwasher rack or bottle tree to drip dry. Siphon your beer from the secondary fermenter to another bucket along with a pre-boiled sugar water solution (this sugar re-activates the yeast to add a little more condition in the bottle). Siphon carefully from here into each bottle. Cap the bottle with sanitised caps (boiling them works fine) and leave at room temperature for at least 2 weeks, more if you have the patience. This conditioning time allows a small build-up of CO_2 to occur naturally.

12 **POUR**

13 **DRINK**

14 **SMILE**

15 **EAT SOME MEAT**

16 AMEN.

CHAPTER

HOW TO...

HOW TO SET UP A GAS GRILL FOR DIRECT AND INDIRECT GRILLING

When you're strapped for time, grilling using gas is the only option. You can use a gas barbecue to grill fast, or smoke low and slow, assuming your grill has a lid.

If possible, close up any big gaps between the grill and lid with sheets of aluminium foil to prevent heat and smoke escaping unnecessarily. Beware not to starve the fire of oxygen and follow all manufacturer's warnings.

DIRECT HEAT OVERVIEW USING 1-ZONE COOKING

Setting up a gas grill for direct cooking is simple. Follow the manufacturer's instructions for lighting the grill. Once lit, let the heat build up for 15 minutes at your desired setting (low, medium or hot) to ensure you have a consistent heat to cook with. Always oil the grates just before grilling. You can do this by dipping half an onion in vegetable oil with some long-handled tongs and using the onion to apply the oil to the grate.

INDIRECT HEAT OVERVIEW USING 2-ZONE COOKING

Again, we usually recommend using charcoal for indirect cooking, but if you only have access to a gas grill and you want to cook a low and slow recipe, then so be it. You'll need a gas grill with a lid, at least 2 burners and possibly a spare gas bottle.

Follow the manufacturer's instructions for lighting the grill. Once lit, let the heat build up for 15 minutes. To convert your gas grill into an indirect heat system, you need to turn off the outside (or front or back) burner or burners so you have a 2-zone set up. To add smoke to the converted system, double-wrap soaked wood chips in aluminium foil, puncture the package a few times and place it directly over one of the fire-up burners. You'll need a few wood chip packages ready for when the smoke dies down.

HOW TO SET UP A CHARCOAL GRILL FOR DIRECT AND INDIRECT GRILLING

For the method described below we have assumed use of a kettle grill, which has a lid. Having a lid is essential if you want to use the smokehouse method.

It's a good idea to build a cooler zone into your blanket of coals by leaving a space completely clear of coals. This will create an area you can move meat to in case you get flare-ups.

DIRECT HEAT OVERVIEW USING 1-ZONE COOKING

Light some lumpwood coals using a chimney. While these are catching fire, place more lumpwood coals on the bottom of your barbecue, then place the coals from the chimney on top of the unlit ones. Wait for all the coals to ash over, put your grilling grate in place and you're ready to start. Add coal little and often to maintain and regulate the heat if you plan to cook for any longer than 2 hours.

INDIRECT HEAT OVERVIEW
USING 2-ZONE COOKING

Follow the same process for 1-zone cooking, but when your coals have ashed over, push the coals over to one half of the kettle grill. This means you'll have direct heat over the coals, and indirect heat over the half that contains no coals. Never split the coals to either side of the grill. This will burn your food during the smoking process, as it's too intense. Carefully place a disposable aluminium pan next to the coals in the indirect half of the grill. This acts as a drip tray and also helps maintain an even temperature from the coal side. Make sure you can top up this pan easily with water throughout the cooking time, as it will begin to evaporate. Add 3-4 chunks of soaked wood to the coal pile. Soaking wood chunks will help them smoulder and smoke, rather than flare up. Position the top grill grate in place and add another, smaller disposable aluminium pan above the coal side. This will also help maintain even temperatures. Don't believe anyone who says that the addition of the water pan is for moisture. It isn't. It's for temperature control.

Having this 2-zone set up is great for smoking low and slow, plus it's good for crisping up things like BBQ chicken or ribs once they've been smoked.

HOW TO SET UP A SMOKER FOR INDIRECT HEAT

Once you have taken the step to invest in a smoker, you'll soon figure out how to regulate the heat and smoke to suit your equipment. Manufactured smokers are either based on the 'bullet' design or the 'offset' design, the most popular being the bullet design made by Weber called the Smokey Mountain (WSM), although there are other cost-effective brands making their way to your local DIY shop and even the high street.

Bullet smokers range in price from £80-£800, and you generally get what you pay for. The 'bullet' has a vertical design, and includes a large water pan between the fire and the grills to regulate heat. The offset smoker design has a smoke chamber and an offset firebox, which uses convection to push smoke and heat from the firebox into one side of the smoke chamber at the lowest entry point, over and under the food and out the other side using a chimney at the highest exit point. Walter, our custom-made mobile smoker, is based on an offset design. If you prefer not to commission one that can feed 500 hungry mites in one serving, then we'd recommend something like a Landmann Grand Tennessee smoker, which costs less than £400 online.

HOW TO MAKE A GRIDIRON AND FIRE FOR CABRITO ASADO

If you decide to make your own gridiron, make sure you use safe materials such as stainless steel, and that you sterilise the finished product before you secure the animal to it. Placing the finished gridiron directly over a hot fire will help burn off any unwanted remnants from the manufacturing process, plus it'll kill most bacteria at the same time.

For our gridiron we used a vertical bar 150cm tall and cross bars 100cm wide. The cross bars need to move up and down the vertical bar, and will need wing bolt type/ grommet type connections on them so they can grip to the vertical bar.

YOU'LL NEED

charcoal and hardwood logs

about 10-15 bricks

hammer

100cm metal tubing which the gridiron bars can slot into, in the ground

gridiron (see intro, above)

hot water and sanitiser solution

sterilised metal wire for securing the goat to the gridiron

wire cutters/pliers

clean and sterilised spray bottle for spritzing

1 Clear a safe area in your back garden to prepare a hot fire on the ground with charcoal and hardwood logs. If it's windy, make sure you have enough space downwind to place the splayed goat so that the heat from the fire is directed towards the goat. You'll need around 4.5 metres of clear space and no nearby fire hazards, such as petrol stations, to be really safe. It's also a good idea to create a barrier around the fire using bricks, leaving one side clear of bricks where you'll be placing the gridiron on (usually downwind). This will prevent the fire from spreading.

2 Before the fire gets too hot, prepare the exact location of where you will be placing the gridiron into the ground. Using a hammer, bash the metal tube deep into the ground, at least 60cm deep, at an angle between 45-60 degrees. The plan is to 'hang' the beast over the fire so that it cooks indirectly from the heat of the fire. Make sure this tubing is really secure, otherwise it'll be a disaster! If you don't have access to the perfect fitting tubing, you can just drive the bottom of the gridiron directly into the ground. If so, do this now, so you don't have to create a pilot hole when the goat is attached to the gridiron.

3 Prepare the gridiron and sterilise with hot water and sanitiser solution. Sterilise the flexible wire and wire cutters too and set aside in a clean area. Turn to page 118 for the Cabrtio Asado recipe.

HOW TO MAKE A JERKY BOX

Before you can make jerky, you'll need to knock up a drying cabinet, or you could just buy one. Commercial desiccators, dryers and dehydrators are available online (if you don't have a South African shop near you) and come in various sizes. If you do buy a commercial dryer, select one that has at least 5-kg capacity. Dehydrators tend to be aimed at drying foodstuffs flat, such as fruit, but can also be used for jerky drying. Purists prefer to hang jerky, and that's the way we do it in our restaurants, although we use bespoke cabinets made of mild steel and glass for some extra theatre.

Drying jerky requires dry heat, and with the use of a simple lightbulb at the bottom of a cardboard box, you can create the right convection environment to hang your own jerky. Essentially, you are aiming to create a chimney effect that sends the dry, warm airflow upwards and over the hanging cured meat. The box can be made of wood or cardboard, but a wooden box will certainly last longer. You also may want to cover the holes in the box with insect netting (the kind used on screen doors). This will stop bugs from getting to your jerky before you do. Here's how to build an entry-level drying box.

The diagram shows a box with a panel that divides the box into two sections, called A and B. Section A is high enough for a 100W or 60W bulb to fit into. Section B is where you will hang the meat. Near the top of section B are wooden or steel rods, which the meat will hang from. There are holes of 1-2.5cm in diameter drilled along the sides of section A, in the divider and in the roof of the box.

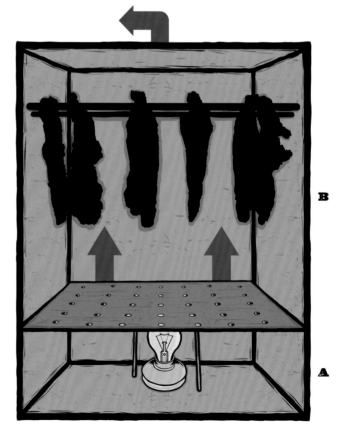

Wood panels to build a box 1m high
x 60cm wide x 60cm deep

Door hinges

Wood dividing panel 60cm x 60cm

Drill with wooden bit

7 wood or metal hanging rods

Plastic-coated paper clips

100W or 60W lightbulb and fitting

HOW IT WORKS

The bulb heats the air in section A. The air rises through the holes in the
divider, through section B, and out the top. The air in section A that has risen
out the top is replaced by air being sucked in through the holes in the sides of
section A. The blue arrows show the airflow.

HOW TO MAKE IT

1 Make a wooden box that measures roughly 1m high x 60cm wide x 60cm
deep, with a door on one side.

2 Place a wooden divider in the box, leaving about 30cm space between the
bottom of the divider and the bottom of the box. Bear in mind that it must
be far enough away from the bottom that you can place the bulb under it.

3 Drill several holes, about 1-2.5cm in diameter, in the sides of section A, in
the divider and in the top of the box.

5 Place about 7 wooden rods inside the box about 5cm from the top. Space
them about 8-10cm apart.

6 Fix the lightbulb in the centre of section A.

7 Hang your meat from the rods using the paper clips, making sure the
pieces don't touch each other (the meat will rot at the spots where they
touch). How long it takes for the meat to dry will depend on the type of
meat, the thickness and the atmospheric conditions at the time, so wait
patiently. See pages 67-71 to find out how to make your own jerky.

HOW TO MAKE A CUBAN-STYLE
PIG ROASTER

A pig roast is a traditional family feast in Cuba and the Cubans know how to build a good simple roaster. They make an outside oven from bricks, place hot coals on the base and position a flattened pig, caged between a lattice of metal bars, on top. This does the job, but some people then add a cover over the pig to help retain heat in the 'oven'. This cooks the beast quicker and crackles the skin a little easier. Installing a cover can be as simple as running some tin foil across the top from one side to the other. We prefer, though, to use a purpose-built stainless-steel cover that doubles up as a tray to house more hot coals, this time directly on top of the oven.

YOU'LL NEED

2 large racks

60 breezeblocks or large bricks

stainless-steel lid

large cool box, to fit the pig

5 bags of ice

pan large enough to hold the pig, with handles for carrying

lumpwood charcoal

metal garden spade

large tray to hold charcoal in pig roaster

wire to build cage for housing the pig

wire cutters

pliers

digital probe thermometer

large mop brush

large wooden picnic table

enough sturdy, clean plastic sheeting to cover a picnic table

First, ask your local fabricator to build you two large racks made of steel rods, preferably stainless steel. This should be about 1200mmm x 2000mm in size, using 12mm rods. We used 5 rods vertically and 8 horizontally to get the right proportions. The flattened pig is sandwiched between them and secured with sterilised wire so you can flip it during the cooking process to cook both sides. To save money, you could make the racks yourself, using plumbing materials to create a large rectangle shape and looping in thick wire in the form of a lattice to secure the pig. Again, you'll need two racks. Be careful to use food-safe materials when making your own pig racks.

Once the pig racks are ready, it's time to build the roaster. This is a simple collection of bricks or breeze blocks placed together to create an oven shape that fits your racks perfectly. The racks need to perch on top of the oven sides, so getting the measurements correct from the outset is important.

Start by figuring out now many base bricks you'll need. These are the bricks that will form the bottom of the pig roaster and are placed directly on the ground, horizontally. Slim bricks are fine here, so we opted for breezeblocks with dimensions of 10 x 21.5 x 44cm. We used about 30 base blocks and set 14 additional thinner ones aside for later use. If you are planning on building the pig roaster on level ground, you may not need to build a base, but it does protect your lawn from burning. Make sure you place the base bricks with the thinnest side down to get the most coverage.

Once you know how many base bricks you need, work on the vertical (wall) brick count. We opted for slightly thicker blocks, 21.5 x 21.5 x 44cm, and used 37 of these to build the walls of the oven. When building the walls of the roaster, make sure you overlap the blocks or bricks in the traditional interleaved way. This keeps the walls are sturdy so they won't fall inwards or outwards if pressure is applied when placing the rack containing the pig on top of them. Build the walls to a height of about 90-120cm above the ground, so the pig isn't placed too close to the hot coals on the base level.

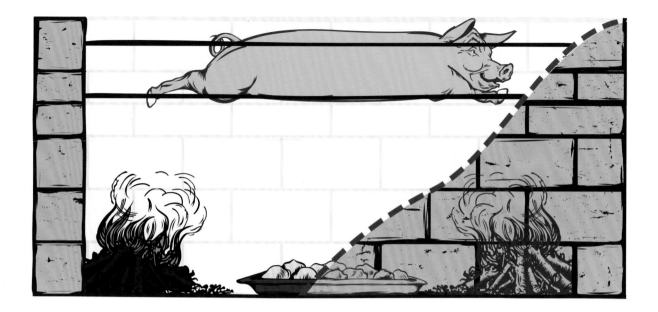

To make sure the racks fit perfectly on the walls, build one complete layer of bricks for all four walls, then place one of the racks on to the single layer of bricks to ensure the walls are all being constructed in the correct positions. You want the rack to perch just under halfway over the inside half of each brick of the 4 walls, leaving space for placing some thinner bricks (same as the base bricks) on the outside half to create a natural stand if you plan to use a lid. When building the walls, make sure the bricks fit tightly together to keep any gaps between the bricks to a minimum.

Once the 4 walls are the right height and they're secure, place one of the racks on top of your roaster to make sure the racks still fit as you intended when you measured up earlier. The rack should rest on the inside half of the bricks of the walls. If you want a lid, it'll need to be made from stainless steel to dimensions larger than the roaster so it can fit on top and over the sides. Our fabricator built a lid measuring 125 x 205cm, giving half a metre each way to play with.

Assuming you have the cover ready, place one of the racks on to the roaster and grab a few (about 14) of the base bricks (the thinner ones). Place these bricks, tallest side up this time, on the outside of the thicker, vertical wall bricks. This will create a mini wall around and above the racks containing the pig so that you can place the lid over the roaster. If you are not planning to use a purpose-built lid, building this mini wall is still useful as it makes it easy to cover the roaster with foil. If you don't build the mini wall element, then you can place the tin foil directly over the pig rack to retain heat in the oven.

That's it. You now have a pig roaster for your next family feast! Before you store them away for the winter, be sure to oil the racks with vegetable oil to prevent them from rusting. Turn to page 122 for the recipe.

HOW TO SET UP YOUR
HOMEBREW KIT

Depending on budget there are a variety of options for your homebrew equipment. Homebrewing is a science, but a fun one! First thing to remember is cleanliness and sterilisation - yeast is a living organism and will feed off anything. Secondly, temperature control is important, so insulating your vessels one way or another is a good idea. An entry-level homebrew kit can be purchased complete (including ingredients) for £25-£50. As you progress from powdered flavourings to 'all-grain', the price goes up along with the quality. To make your own homebrew IPA, see page 232.

THERMOMETERS

Of course, you can rely on adhesive thermometer strips, but the best option is a food-grade temperature probe.

SUNDRIES

The type you need depends on your chosen style of brewkit - consult your local homebrew shop for advice on the valves, caps, stoppers and tubing that you will need.

MASH TUN

This will hold the grain and hot water at temperature. It can be made in different ways but a 22-litre bucket with a false bottom (a mesh at the bottom with drainage) will be the cheapest. False bottoms are cheap, and easy to install, or you can make your own. To make your own, get a 30cm toilet water line with stainless braiding and cut the ends off. Remove the stainless braid. Crimp one end closed with pliers and attach the other end to a 9.5mm (3/8in) flex copper piece with a hose clamp. Use a drilled rubber stopper where the hole is near the bottom of the cooler to prevent leaking. A valve or vinyl hose clamp can be used to control the flow of your hot liquor after the mash.

SPARGING

This is the process of rinsing the hot liquor off the grain bed, and will require a length of hose and connections so you can circulate run-off back on top of the malt.

'THE COPPER': BOILING

This needs to be a container that will hold at least 25 litres of liquid, and can be heated. You can get brewing-specific containers ranging from £80- £200, in plastic or metal.

WORT CHILLER

You can purchase a wort chiller for about £100, but it is unnecessary if you have boiled less than 12 litres. Without a chiller you can still get good results by placing the wort boiling pot into an ice bath, either in a large sink, or the bathtub.

FERMENTERS

The cheapest is a 25-litre bucket with an airlock on the top. An airlock is a device that only lets air out and not in. You will need at least TWO fermenters (primary and secondary) and a siphon for the transfer between the two.

BOTTLES, CASKS OR KEGS

You can source these from a local or online homebrew retailer. For bottles, you'll require caps and a 'crown capper' to seal the bottles. For kegs, you'll need a CO_2 and some additional keg-filling equipment and sundries, but even these won't cost more than £100 (the kegs themselves can be expensive, but of course everything is re-usable!). Plastic casks can be bought new for less than £30.

OVEN TEMPERATURE CONVERSION CHART

Celsius	Farenheit	Gas Mark
95°	200°	0
110°	225°	¼
120°	250°	½
140°	275°	1
150°	300°	2
170°	325°	3
180°	350°	4
190°	375°	5
200°	400°	6
220°	425°	7
230°	450°	8
245°	475°	9

INGREDIENTS GLOSSARY

Ancho chiles

This is the dried version of the poblano pepper. Ancho chiles have a deep red colour and a wrinkled skin. Anchos are sweet and smoky with a flavour slightly reminiscent of raisins. This is a mild pepper which falls into the 1,000-250,000 Scoville heat chart range.

Baby back ribs

This cut of pork rib is considered to be the most tender as it comes from the top/back of the pig. This rib cut contains part of the loin, often found on back bacon.

Beef long

Cut from the short rib of the cow, a.k.a Jacob's Ladder. Ask your butcher for whole short rib, but not to use the bandsaw to cut them down.

Bird's eye

A tiny but very hot pepper, somewhere in the 100,000-225,000 Scoville heat chart range.

Brisket HOF

This refers to the 'Hunk Of Flat', which is the leaner section of a whole brisket that contains two muscles

Brisket HOP

This refers to the 'Hunk Of Point', which is the fattier and, some say, more tasty section of the brisket that contains two muscles.

Bullet smoker

Shaped like a bullet, this smoker is like an elongated kettle grill, but is used mainly for indirect smoking. Available at most hardware supermarkets.

Buttermilk

Slightly sour to the taste, this is the remaining milky by-product after butter has been churned.

Cabrito

Young goat meat.

Canoe-cut marrow bones

From the shin, these bones are shaped like guttering, and perfect for luging bourbon.

Cedar plank

Used for smoking fish, this wood provides an earthy flavour profile.

Cherry Bitters

Similar to Angostura, but with the addition of cherry sweetness.

Chipotle

Smoked ripened jalapenos.

Chuck Steak

Used to make our burgers, we use a mix of 20% fat, 80% beef

Tomahawk steak

The daddy of steaks, huge in size and found on the end of a huge bone. Perfect for 'dirty grilling' and are usually over 1kg in weight per steak.

Country ribs

These are not really ribs. They are cut from the front end of the baby backs.

Cracklings

Pure pig skin, cut into cubes and fried. Great as a snack, especially with beer.

Cruibins

Stuffed pig's trotters favoured by the Irish.

Dirty mayo

This is a seasoned mayonnaise-based product which adds a spicy, herby and salty kick to sandwiches and burgers.

Dirty sauce
This is the epic burger and sandwich sauce that contains 28 proprietary ingredients we use in the restaurant

Ghost
a.k.a. Naga or Bhut Jolokia, this is an EXTREMELY hot pepper. Use with extreme caution and always wash hands after handling. This pepper contains over 1,000,000 Scoville units.

Habañero
A very, very hot pepper which hails from Mexico, somewhere in the 100,000-350,000 Scoville heat chart range.

Hog skins
Pig intestine casings used for making sausage which come in different sizes - large and medium.

Horlicks
This is a malted drink brand often in powder form. You can use other brands such as Ovaltine or supermarket own brands.

Hotlink
A Texas smoked sausage favourite sometimes called "Hot Guts" that contains fatty ground beef and/or pork laced with cayenne, garlic and mustard. You're best off making these or asking your butcher to, as they're not widely available in the UK.

Jalapeño
A mature jalapeño chilli is 5-10 cm (2.0-3.9 in) long, and is commonly picked and consumed while still green, but occasionally it is allowed to fully ripen and turn crimson red. This is a medium hot pepper which falls into the 2,500-10,000 Scoville heat chart range.

Jerky
This cured, then dried lean meat is best when homemade, but is available in most supermarkets. Beef is more popular, but game jerky is awesome if you can find it. Look out for the South African version, biltong.

Kansas City BBQ sauce
Sweet and smoky tomato-based sauce, probably the most recognised and popular BBQ the globe knows.

Kettle grill
Made famous by Weber, this is a round barbecue base with a tight fitting round lid which has inbuilt air dampers which allow for direct and indirect grilling and smoking.

Leaf gelatin
These come in clear paper-thin leaves, but you can use gelatin powder sachets if you can't find the leaves.

Lexington Dipper
This is a thin, vinegary, and hot dipping sauce favoured in the Lexington area of North Carolina.

Mojo
This spicy sauce usually made from olive oil, salt, water, chili peppers, garlic, paprika, cumin or coriander and other spices originated in the Canary Islands, but it is very popular in Central and South America.

Molasses
Also known as black treacle, a by-product of sugar creation in liquid form (with a high viscosity).

Monterey Jack
An American cheese, sometimes seen as 'Jack Cheese'. Great for burgers.

North Carolina BBQ sauce
A sweet and tangy vinegar-based sauce with a little chili flake kicker.

Old Bay seasoning
A branded crab seasoning from Maryland, USA.

Pork butt
This is a US term for a pork shoulder. You may also hear the term Boston butt, which is the same. This cut has the hand removed from the shoulder but does contain the shoulder blade.

Prague Powder #1
This is a curing salt that is used in food preservation to prevent or slow spoilage by bacteria or fungus. It is used for pickling meats as part of the process to make sausage or cured meat and contains 6% sodium nitrite and 94% table salt.

Rib tips
Often called 'dog meat', these are the featherbone trimmings removed from the larger pork spare rib sheet. You can find rib tips towards the top of the belly ribs cut from your butcher.

Scotch Bonnet
A very, very hot pepper, originally from the Caribbean is sometimes sweet, but falls somewhere in the 100,000-225,000 Scoville heat chart range.

Sheep skins
Smaller in diameter sausage casings used to make jerky sausage.

Silverside
Beef cut from the hindquarter. This is our preferred cut for making beef jerky. It's readily available from your local butcher.

South Carolina BBQ sauce
a.k.a. Carolina Gold, this is a mild mustard-based BBQ sauce with a little brown sugar for balance.

Spare ribs
This is whole sheet of pork ribs that combine the St Louis cut and rib tips. You can often find whole sheet spare ribs from Chinese food wholesalers but they will be frozen.

St Louis cut
This style of rib is trimmed from a larger pork spare rib cut, which removes all the annoying grisly featherbones, leaving only pure awesome meat for you to bite on. This rib cut should have around 14 bones and is

USDA
United States Department of Agriculture, who test and approve premium cuts of meat such as brisket.

Vodka Infusion
Also known as 'fat-washing', this is the process of adding rendered meat fat such as bacon or lamb to a bottle of liquor, mixing it through the alcohol and then freezing it. Once the fat solidifies, the alcohol which has taken on the flavour of the meat is then decanted and used for awesome cocktails.

Weaner pig
A pig from the age of weaning until they reach about 40 pounds in weight.

Wild Turkey
The best house bourbon we've found!

INDEX

ACKNOWLEDGEMENTS

To our families at home with thanks for their continued patience and understanding, without you all, we'd be nothing. To our Red's family, thanks for all your hard work and attention to detail, we're eternally grateful. To all our amazing customers who eat, drink and party at Red's every week - keep coming and we'll keep smoking. To all the beautiful beasts who lived their lives just waiting to sleep in our smokers.

THEN ALL THESE GUYS:

Rob, Jimmy, Jill and Keith our butchers, Luke fl Ilkley Brewery, John 'Weird' Beard, Craig Thorpe (peanut butter chocolate cheesecake recipe), James Newman, for making James's life easier, Greg Nash for making everyone's lives better, Sven van Bizzle, Leelex Bars - you watered us when no one else would, Toby Shea, Kath Arkell, Vincent at Rosebud's Lil' Joes BBQ for the awesome photos. Pilgrimage people: Moose, Melissa, Daniel Vaughn, Pecan Lodge, Snow's BBQ, Richard fl Whole Hog, Brett at Louis Mueller, Xanax Twins and the Austin Globetrotters, the Donnie Sports Network, the Dallas Jet Washers, David Gest, Sleepy James, that woman who drove us to Austin from that river place on the last night, John Emery from Jack Stack BBQ,

Wild Turkey and Jimmy Mav fl Normans, and City Home for putting up with our noise and hot sauce antics. George, Steve, Phil, Jobs Jones street for the CPUs and tech hook-ups, Jamie, Dave and Tone at Vapour for reinventing neon, James Askham at the creative genius that is Warm, Sanderling Estates for giving us our first chance with a location, Pat Miller for selling pigs lips in the first place, Derek Rettel, Dan Schieler and Mike O'Brien, Peter Martin,

Mark Wingett, Distorted Productions, Ben Marsh, Brandon 'Colombo' Stephens, Andrew Turf without whom we wouldn't know Brandon, Luke Johnson, we've name dropped you loads, Adam Richman you never call us back, Lauren at Four Corners Brewing Company, Honey French and Yiannis (World Famous Hickory's), Louise Greenwell (PR), Phil Lynas and the team at All About Food, Chritine Moir and the gang at Jigsaw Foods, National Vegetarian Week and the ASA, F**k You Hanson, The Matte Gray Band, UGK (front, back, side to side!), Big D BBQ Battle and the Dallas PD, Stu, Liam & Bupa at Teabag Digital, Alex Simmons, JJB and the team at Rugby AM, Kappa for keeping all our doors in order, Jordan and Josh - never had a bad night!, Antony Cotton, Rufus Hound, Matt Lewis, Ian Kirke and the rest of the Leeds Rhinos team, Steve Allison for originally introducing Scott and James,

Vivienne Clore and Nick Canham. This Morning and Sunday Brunch for letting us on the telly, Tommy and Juliette Jowitt for the use of your gardens all the time, John and Dodge for clearing up our mess in the gardens all the time, John Berry and the team at Dawnvale for making random roasters and pig pans. And finally, Amanda, Jillian and Jinny who believed in the first Red's True Barbecue recipe book.

To all our hungry, BBQ-loving believers for allowing us the opportunity to have the best job in the world.

This edition first published in Great Britain in 2015 by
Orion, an imprint of the Orion Publishing Group Ltd
Orion House, 5 Upper St Martin's Lane,
London WC2H 9EA
An Hachette UK Company

1 3 5 7 9 10 8 6 4 2

A CIP catalogue record for this book is available from the British Library.

ISBN: 9781 4091 5635 2

Designer:	Warm
Photographer:	James Brown Photography
Food and prop stylist:	Rob Morris
Editor:	Jinny Johnson
Project editor:	Jillian Young
Copy editor:	Laura Nickoll
Proofreader:	Jenny Wheatly
Indexer:	Rosemary Dear

Printed in China

The Orion Publishing Group's policy is to use papers that are natural, renewable and recyclable and made from wood grown in sustainable forests. The logging and manufacturing processes are expected to conform to the environmental regulations of the country of origin.

Every effort has been made to fulfil requirements with regard to reproducing copyright material. The author and publisher will be glad to rectify any omissions at the earliest opportunity.

www.orionbooks.co.uk

by BOOK or by COOK
COOKING
EATING
SHARING

For lots more delicious recipes plus articles, interviews and videos from the best chefs cooking today visit our blog
bybookorbycook.co.uk

Follow us
 @bybookorbycook

Find us
 facebook.com/bybookorbycook